The Closest Race of 2016

Issa v. Applegate in California's 49th Congressional District

MATTHEW J. DALE

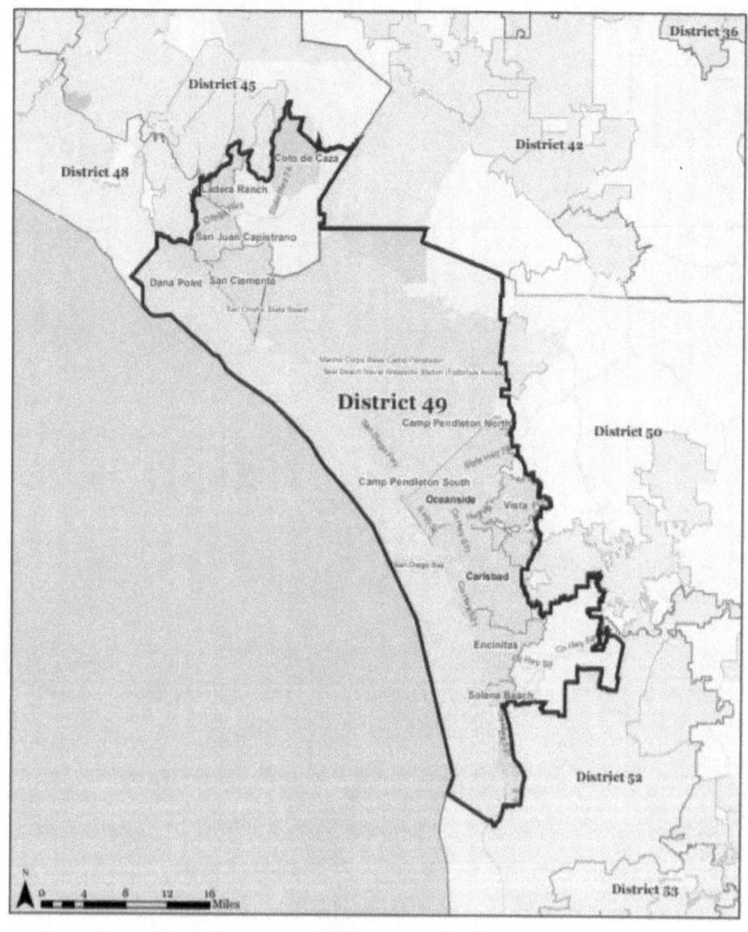

District 36
District 45
District 42
District 48
Coto de Caza
Ladera Ranch
San Juan Capistrano
Dana Point
San Clemente
San Onofre State Beach
Marine Corps Base Camp Pendleton
Seal Beach Naval Weapons Station (Fallbrook Annex)
District 49
Camp Pendleton North
District 50
Camp Pendleton South
Oceanside
Vista
San Diego Bay
Carlsbad
Encinitas
Solana Beach
District 52
District 53
N
0   4   8   12   16
Miles

CONTENTS

INTRODUCTION

National, state, and local politics combined to have a much more significant impact on California's 49th Congressional District in 2016 than any other congressional district. The Republican incumbent, Darrell Issa, had been a high-profile critic of President Obama during his time as chairman of the House Oversight Committee. After Donald Trump secured the Republican presidential nomination, Congressman Issa associated himself early and often with the candidate. The Democratic challenger, Colonel Doug Applegate, was a first-time candidate for elected office and politically more aligned with Senator Bernie Sanders than Hillary Clinton. It was also the closest House race in the country that year.

This book will examine the district, the campaign strategies, and the issues that influenced them. Both candidates' connection to the district and national political movements impacted their standing with the voters in the district, and donors nationwide. Mythologies of the election are identified and evaluated. The timeline of events starts December 5th, 2014, the day Congressman Issa declared his candidacy, and ends December 2nd, 2016, the day Colonel Applegate conceded the race.

CHAPTER 1: THE DISTRICT

California's 49th Congressional District, represented by Congressman Issa in 2016, was last redrawn in 2011. The district stretches from the southern coastal region of Orange County to the northern edge of La Jolla in San Diego County. Cities fully within the district are Dana Point, San Juan Capistrano, and San Clemente in Orange County and Carlsbad, Del Mar, Encinitas, Oceanside, Solana Beach, and Vista in San Diego County. Marine Corps Base Camp Pendleton and the San Onofre Nuclear Plant are also within the district.[1] These boundaries were used in the 2012, 2014, and 2016 general elections.

---

[1] State of California Citizens Redistricting Commission. "Final Report on 2011 Redistricting." August 15th, 2011.

In the first report on voter registration since the district was redrawn, registered Republicans outnumbered registered Democrats by more than 50,000 voters. Registered Republicans accounted for 42.7% of the district's electorate, whereas registered Democrats accounted for only 28.6%. Assuming voters registered with a major party voted along partisan lines, a Democrat candidate would need to attract almost 75% of non-aligned voters to win. In all of California, 43.6% of voters were registered with the Democratic Party, while only 30.3% were registered with the Republican Party. The Democratic Party had a 2.2 million voter registration advantage over the Republican Party throughout the state.[2]

Culturally, the 49th Congressional District is unique in that it covers parts of both Orange County and San Diego County. The political culture in these two counties has historically leaned Republican. From 1948 to 2004, San Diego County only voted for a Democrat presidential candidate once; Bill Clinton won the county with only 37% of the vote in 1992. Orange County voted for the Republican presidential candidate in every election from 1940 to 2012. Orange County was the birthplace of President Richard

---

[2] California Secretary of State. Report of Registration by Congressional District: January 3rd, 2012.

Nixon. During President Nixon's time in office, San Clemente was the site of his "Western White House." President Ronald Reagan announced his re-election bid in 1984 at the Mile Square Park in Fountain Valley. The 1996 Republican National Convention was held in San Diego. In 2014, San Diego became the largest city in the United States with a Republican mayor. The largest annual gathering of Republican activists in Orange County is the Flag Day Salute. In San Diego County, the largest annual gathering of Republican activists is the Lincoln Reagan Dinner.

In the 2012 presidential election, Republican candidate Mitt Romney won the district with 52.2% of the vote, or 153,856 votes. President Obama received 45.7% of the vote, or 134,447 votes.[3] President Obama won the state with 60.2% of the vote.[4] In that election, Congressman Issa was re-elected after winning 58.2% of the vote. He received 159,725 votes, meaning more people voted for Congressman Issa than Mitt Romney. The Democrat challenger received 114,893 votes, meaning about twenty thousand people that voted for President Obama did not vote for the

---

[3] California Secretary of State. 2012 General Election Supplement to the Statement of Vote: Counties by Congressional Districts for President.
[4] California Secretary of State. 2012 General Election Statement of Vote: President.

Democrat congressional candidate.[5] This relationship between the top and bottom of the ballot would have an important impact on the 2016 general election, as well.

As of the 2014 primary election registration close date, the 49th Congressional District had 362,406 registered voters, of which 146,764 were Republicans and 104,641 were Democrats.[6] Republicans had a 42,000 voter registration advantage. The Republican advantage had declined because 2,593 more voters registered with the Democratic Party, whereas 5,668 voters left the Republican Party (or the district) since the previous primary, in 2012.

In the primary election on June 3rd, 2014, four candidates competed, including Congressman Issa. Dave Peiser and Noboru Isagawa appeared on the ballot as Democrat candidates. One other candidate competed as a write-in Democrat candidate. In total, 91,407 votes were cast. Congressman Issa received 61.9% of the vote, followed by Dave Peiser at 28.4%, so they advanced to the general election. In the portion of the district that belongs to Orange County, Congressman Issa won with almost 70.0% of the vote.

---

[5] California Secretary of State. 2012 General Election Statement of Vote: United States Representative.
[6] California Secretary of State. Report of Registration by Congressional District: May 19th, 2014.

He also won in the portion that belongs to San Diego, but only with 59.4%.[7]

The 49th Congressional District aligns most closely with the 36th State Senate District, which mostly overlaps with the 73rd State Assembly District and the 76th State Assembly District. Republican incumbent Senator Pat Bates was the only candidate to appear on the ballot. She received 88,171 votes, or 99.1% of the total.[8] Five Republicans, and no one else, appeared on the ballot in the primary to represent the 73rd State Assembly District. Republican incumbent Assemblyman Rocky J. Chavez was the only candidate to appear on the ballot in the primary to represent the 76th State Assembly District. He received 40,764 votes, or 99.9% of the vote.[9]

On the 2014 general election registration close date, of the 361,569 registered voters in the 49th Congressional District, 145,264 were registered with the Republican Party and 104,193 were registered with the Democratic Party.[10] The Republican voter

---

[7] California Secretary of State. 2014 Primary Election Statement of Vote: United States Representative.

[8] California Secretary of State. 2014 Primary Election Statement of the Vote: State Senator by District.

[9] California Secretary of State. 2014 Primary Election Statement of the Vote: State Assemblymember by District.

[10] California Secretary of State. Report of Registration by Congressional District: October 20th, 2014.

registration advantage had declined to 41,000 voters. Although the overall number of registered voters declined between the 2012 general election and the 2014 general election, only 5,322 voters left the Democratic Party (or the district), whereas 12,548 voters left the Republican Party (or the district).

In the 2014 general election, Congressman Issa won the district, with 60.2% of the vote, against Democrat Dave Peiser, receiving 39.8%. A total of 163,142 votes were counted. Congressman Issa did better in the portion of the district that covers Orange County, where he won with 68.7% of the vote.[11] Higher turnout among Orange County Republicans would also compensate for lower turnout among San Diego County Democrats in the 2016 general election.

Democrat candidates won all state-wide partisan elections in 2014. Republican Pete Peterson, a candidate for Secretary of State, performed the best of all Republican candidates, but only received 46.4% of the vote. The Republican candidate for governor only received 40.0% of the vote.[12]

Going into the 2016 election, the 49th Congressional District was leaning less towards the

---

[11] California Secretary of State. 2014 General Election Statement of the Vote: United States Representative.
[12] California Secretary of State. 2014 General Election Statement of the Vote: Summary Pages.

Republican Party in a state that was shifting even more towards the Democratic Party.

CHAPTER 2: THE CONTEST BEGINS

Congressman Issa signed his Statement of Candidacy for the 2016 election on December 5th, 2014. His campaign committee, Issa for Congress, had over $3.7 million cash on hand at the end of 2014.[13]

As the new year began, so did a new era for the Orange County Republican Party. Over a thirty-year period, the local party only had two chairmen. The *Orange County Register* described Scott Baugh, the retiring chairman, as a "charismatic former state Assembly GOP leader," and described Tom Fuentes, the previous chairman, as "a must-see guy for national Republican elites visiting the county," with "a political network that extended to the White

---

[13] Filing FEC-986813. Form 3: Year-End. Filed January 27th, 2015.

House." Fred Whitaker, the incoming chairman, was described as "a relatively unknown GOP foot soldier."[14] Henry Vandermeir, the Chairman of the Democratic Party of Orange County, had been in his position since 2013.

The California Secretary of State reported voter registration by congressional district on February 10th, 2015. The 49th Congressional District had 361,945 registered voters, of which 144,883 were Republicans and 104,027 were Democrats.[15] Republicans had a 40,000 voter registration advantage. Compared to the first report of voter registration after redistricting in 2011, Democrat registrations had increased 1.3%, Republican registrations had decreased 5.3%, and other or non-partisan registrations combined had increased 10.6%.

In the first quarter of 2015, the campaign was more focused on monetary affairs than voter outreach. The campaign committee's largest expense in the three months ended March 31, 2015 was tax payments on interest. With so much cash on hand, the campaign committee had accrued over $71,000 in taxes on interest income payable to the U.S. Treasury

---

[14] Wisckol, Martin. "GOP Foot Soldier to Guide County Party." *Orange County Register*. January 18th, 2015.
[15] California Secretary of State. Report of Registration by Congressional District: February 10th, 2015.

and the California Franchise Tax Board, or tax preparation fees. The second highest expense was over $30,000 in fundraising and media consulting services provided by two vendors. In the three months ended March 31, 2015 Issa for Congress had raised $160,000, spent $219,000, and ended the period with $3.8 million cash on hand.[16]

Ted Cruz, a Republican Senator from Texas, announced his candidacy for president on March 23rd, 2015. Hillary Clinton, the former Secretary of State, announced her candidacy for the Democratic Party presidential nomination on April 12th. The next day, Marco Rubio, a Republican Senator from Florida, announced his candidacy for president. Congressman Issa would later endorse Senator Rubio. Bernie Sanders, the Senator from Vermont, formally announced he planned to seek the Democratic Party presidential nomination on May 26th. On June 16th, Donald Trump promised his supporters "We will make America great again!" More than a dozen other candidates made it to the first televised debate for both parties, but these five candidates ended up being most relevant to the 49th Congressional District.

---

[16] Filing FEC-1003429. Form 3: April Quarterly. Filed April 15th, 2015.

Between April and May of 2015, the San Diego Republican Party hosted presidential straw polls at street fairs throughout the county, and posted results on its Facebook page. At the Encinitas Street Fair, Scott Walker won the Republican Party presidential straw poll with 16.8% of the vote. Marco Rubio came in second place with 16.2% of the vote. Ted Cruz came in fifth place with 3.6% of the vote. At the 20th Annual Fiesta de los Penasquitos, 76 people participated in the Republican Party presidential straw poll. Jeb Bush and Marco Rubio were tied for first place with 18.4% of the vote. Ted Cruz tied with two other candidates for seventh place. At the Carlsbad Street Fair, there were 135 votes cast in the Republican Party presidential straw poll. Scott Walker won with 16.3% of the vote. Marco Rubio came in second place with 11.9% of the vote. Ted Cruz and Donald Trump were tied for sixth place with 8.1% of the vote. At the Escondido Street Fair, Dr. Ben Carson won the Republican Party presidential straw poll with 20% of the vote. Rand Paul came in second place, with 18% of the vote. Ted Cruz and Scott Walker were tied for third place, with 14% of the vote. Marco Rubio and Mike Huckabee were tied for fourth place, with 10% of the vote. At the Valley Center Street Fair, Dr. Ben Carson again won the Republican Party presidential straw poll, with 21.6% of the vote. Ted Cruz and Scott Walker were tied for second place, with 16.2% of the vote. Rand Paul and Marco Rubio were tied for third place, with 13.5% of the vote. Jeb Bush and Donald Trump were tied for fourth place, with 5.4% of the vote. In summary, Scott Walker and Dr. Ben Carson both had the most first-place wins. Neither of them made it to the California primary. Marco Rubio tied for first place once, but came in second place as often as he came in fourth place. Ted Cruz tied for second place once, but also ranked as low as seventh place. The first choices of San Diego Republicans did not align with the eventual first choices of early primary states, such as Iowa and New Hampshire.

In the second quarter of 2015, no opponents had entered the race to challenge Congressman Issa. The campaign's largest expense during this time was printing and postage costs, which exceeded $29,000. This slightly exceeded fees paid for fundraising and media consulting services. A contribution of $5,000 was made to both the Republican Party of Orange County and the Republican Party of San Diego County. As of June 30th, 2015, Issa for Congress had raised $334,000, spent $314,000, and ended the period with $3.8 million cash on hand.

At the 2015 San Diego County Fair in Del Mar, which ran from June 5th to July 5th, over 2,000 people voted in the local Republican Party's presidential straw poll. Marco Rubio won, with 13.1% of the vote. Donald Trump came in fifth place, with 9.6% of the vote and Ted Cruz came in sixth place, with 7.2% of the vote. It should be noted that Donald Trump had not officially announced he was running for president until about half-way through the event, but still beat Senator Cruz.

On July 5th, 2015, Colonel Douglas Applegate filed his Statement of Candidacy. The contest had officially begun. Colonel Applegate went to war armed with his personal email on his candidacy forms and his personal phone number on his campaign website.[17] By the end of the third quarter of 2015, Issa for Congress had raised $379,000, spent $394,000, and had $3.6 million cash on hand.[18] Applegate for Congress had raised $23,000, spent $3,000, and had $19,000 cash on hand.[19]

An editorial in the *San Diego Union-Tribune* declared the arrival of "the summer of our discontent" in the presidential campaign. Hillary

---

[17] Stewart, Joshua. "Darrell Issa takes decisive lead over Doug Applegate to win a ninth term." *San Diego Union-Tribune.* November 29th, 2017.

[18] Filing FEC-1028677. Form 3: October Quarterly. Filed October 15th, 2015.

[19] Filing FEC-1029038. Form 3: October Quarterly. Filed October 15th, 2015.

Clinton's status as the front-runner for the Democratic Party nomination was described as faltering, but the Editorial Board noted "this time the candidate interrupting her progress toward the White House isn't groundbreaking, charismatic, well-funded Barack Obama. It's Vermont Sen. Bernie Sanders, a 73-year-old self-proclaimed socialist whom few had heard of before this year." Donald Trump, labeled a "billionaire celebrity entrepreneur," was accused of "attempting to frame very difficult issues in either-or terms." The candidate's views on immigration were described as "extreme bluster," which "both exaggerates concerns about border security and scapegoats undocumented immigrants for much larger economic problems." His foreign policy stances were described as a "bullying tone and bellicose declarations," that were scary, but "would be far scarier if he actually had a realistic chance of becoming commander-in-chief." The Editorial Board expected, and hoped, that the question of electability would sooner or later drive Donald Trump out of the race.[20]

The next month, the *San Diego Union-Tribune* provided commentary on the second Republican

---

[20] The Editorial Board. "Presidential Politics: The Summer of Our Discontent." *San Diego Union-Tribune.* August 19th, 2015.

presidential candidate debate, held on Wednesday, September 16th, 2015. The Editorial Board acknowledged "there is an immense appetite in the United States for candidates who reject and ridicule the status quo," but called Donald Trump both an imperfect and ridiculous means of satisfying this appetite. The candidate's comments on vaccines were called "dangerously dumb," and his stances on foreign policy were called "clueless," but the newspaper lamented these comments "may somehow endear him even more to his surprisingly broad and durable coalition of supporters." Echoing the previous month's hope that Donald Trump would exit the race, the Editorial Board hoped the confrontation with Carly Fiorina during the debate was "the beginning of the end for the Trump phenomenon." The Editorial Board also claimed it would feel safer after Senator Cruz drops out of the race. The senator from Texas was compared to Greg Stillson, a populist politician in Steven King's 1979 novel "The Dead Zone" who starts a nuclear holocaust, but charitably conceded that Senator Cruz was an Ivy League-educated version. Dr. Ben Carson was described as "affable and pleasant while not particularly commanding or well-informed." The Editorial Board had much more favorable things to say about establishment candidates. It claimed former Governor Jeb Bush "jousted effectively with Trump." It speculated Senator Rubio seemed "close to a lock to be the vice presidential nominee." It claimed Senator Lindsey Graham "came across as in command of the issues and authentically passionate about big issues."[21]

At the September meeting of the San Diego Republican Party, Donald Trump came in first place in the straw poll. Senator Cruz came in fifth place. Vote totals, percentages, and Senator Rubio's results were not disclosed.

Less than one week after the second Republican presidential candidate debate, Wisconsin Governor Scott Walker suspended his bid for the nomination. Governor Walker's stated reason for dropping out was quoted as allowing voters to "focus on a limited number of candidates who can offer a positive conservative alternative to the current front-runner." An editorial in the *San Diego Union-Tribune* confidently declared, "the destructive, divisive Trump campaign will thankfully be finished."[22]

National attention shifted to Congress that week after Republican House Speaker John Boehner

---

[21] The Editorial Board. "On Donald and Carly and Jeb and More." *San Diego Union-Tribune.* September 17th, 2015.
[22] The Editorial Board. "Walker's Exit May Speed the Fall of Trump." *San Diego Union-Tribune.* September 22nd, 2015.

unexpectedly announced he would resign within the next month. The Editorial Board of the *San Diego Union-Tribune* commented that this "reflects the fundamentally strange place the Republican Party is in." Despite the party's success in Congress and at the state level, the Editorial Board claimed "the confrontational approach favored by tea party lawmakers is broadly disliked by the independents, moderates and libertarians who are the swing voters whom Republicans need to win presidential elections." At that point in time, Congressman Kevin McCarthy, a California Republican that represents Bakersfield, was the Majority Leader. He was expected to be the next speaker of the House. The Editorial Board hoped that Congressman McCarthy could use his new clout to fashion drought relief legislation to benefit California. It warned "that the more he accommodates the House GOP's hard-core majority, the less likely it is there will be a Republican in the White House come January 2017."[23] Oddly, the Editorial Board had previously acknowledged that the so-called "confrontational approach" of Senator Sanders, Donald Trump, and Senator Cruz had driven their campaign success.

---

[23] The Editorial Board. "Boehner's Exit Illustrates the GOP's Conundrum." *San Diego Union-Tribune.* September 25th, 2015.

At the 2015 Salute to Republican Elected Officials in San Diego County in October, 220 votes were cast in a presidential straw poll. Marco Rubio came in first place. Donald Trump came in third place. Ted Cruz's performance and percentages were not disclosed.

When Majority Leader McCarthy withdrew as a candidate to be the next House Speaker, the *San Diego Union-Tribune* Editorial Board called it both "stunning" and "an uncommonly selfless political act by a principled politician." His chances "had been weakened by his ill-advised comments earlier this month that were widely interpreted as ascribing crass political motives to the Republican-led Benghazi hearings and Hillary Clinton's role in that tragedy as secretary of state." The Editorial Board claimed House Republicans were now in greater disarray than ever before.[24]

Congressman Paul Ryan, a Wisconsin Republican, was elected House Speaker in late October. The Editorial Board of the *San Diego Union-Tribune* observed that the Republican Party was at a crossroad: "It can either continue to make concessions to its angriest and loudest members—

---

[24] The Editorial Board. "With McCarthy Out, Who Now to Lead the House?" *San Diego Union-Tribune.* October 8th, 2015.

who somehow believe America is failing and who see the federal government as hopelessly corrupt—or it can seek to fashion a modern, constructive conservative agenda that doesn't indulge such fantasies as eliminating Medicare or Social Security or engage in juvenile, futile brinksmanship over extending national debt limits." The Board lamented "three of the four Republican presidential candidates with the best odds going forward embrace this mindless critique of a doomed, listless America and affection for radical tactics." Donald Trump and Dr. Ben Carson were criticized for heaping contempt "on a Washington they depict as run by fools and knaves." Senator Cruz was criticized for, in the Board's view, depicting his opponents as traitors. In contrast, the Board praised Senator Rubio for "hints of interest in what bipartisan coalitions might accomplish in pushing for a 21st-century education system that emphasizes 21st-century job skills, that revamps the tax code in a way that encourages economic growth and that fixes a broken immigration system." In his new role, the Board urged Speaker Ryan to confront the "hardcore flamethrowers in his caucus," and hoped he would fare better than Congressman Boehner.[25] Among 847 registered

---

[25] The Editorial Board. "What Does GOP Hope to Accomplish?"

voters polled by the NBC News/Wall Street Journal Survey between October 25th and 29th of 2015, 45% preferred Republicans have control Congress after the next election, which matched the percent of respondents that preferred Democrats. The remaining 10% were undecided.[26] Despite the leadership turnover, at least one national poll showed voters still viewed the Republican Party as favorably as the Democratic Party.

At the San Diego County Republican Party's October debate watch party, Senator Rubio won first place in the straw poll. Donald Trump came in second place and Senator Cruz came in third place. The San Diego County Republican Party held a straw poll during the November Republican candidate debate watch party. Donald Trump came in first place. Senator Cruz and Senator Rubio were tied for second. Vote total and percentages were not disclosed. Assuming the same people voted in October and November's debate watch party straw polls, then Donald Trump and Senator Cruz gained favorability over Senator Rubio.

On November 24th, the *San Diego Union-Tribune* Editorial Board called Donald Trump a

---

San Diego Union-Tribune. October 30th, 2015.

[26] NBC News/Wall Street Journal Survey. Study #15463. Date Range: October 25th-29th, 2015.

"blowhard billionaire" and claimed his demagoguery reached new highs after claiming there were people cheering from New Jersey as the World Trade Center collapsed on September 11th, 2001. The Editorial Board described Donald Trump as a "deplorable Joseph McCarthy-style scoundrel." It conceded that Donald Trump's views on immigration "play well not just with nativists but with people who wonder how increased immigration will affect income inequality or who are alarmed with what has happened in Europe as nations struggle to integrate new populations with different backgrounds," but called on other Republican candidates to "address these legitimate concerns while also denouncing Trump for his ugly insistence on depicting Muslim-Americans as a fifth column with no loyalties beyond religious ones." If Donald Trump is not stopped, the Editorial Board warned, "he will be looked back on as someone who defined modern Republicanism to millions of impressionable voters as mean, dishonest and hallucinatory." A parallel was drawn between the national Republican Party and the California Republican Party. In 1994, Republican Governor Pete Wilson supported Proposition 187, which prohibited illegal aliens from using many state services. The consequence, claimed the Editorial Board, was "to define the state GOP as anti-minority and to help make its candidates for statewide office perpetual long shots." It admitted the parallel was not precise, but nevertheless claimed toleration for Donald Trump risked the Republican Party becoming "a natural haven for knaves and fools."[27]

Congressman Issa formally endorsed Senator Rubio for the Republican presidential nomination on November 30th, 2015.[28] A CBS poll published November 22nd, 2015 for the upcoming first-in-the-nation Iowa caucus showed Senator Rubio had 11% support, which was fourth place behind Donald Trump, Senator Cruz, and Dr. Ben Carson.[29] A Quinnipiac University poll published on November 24th, 2015 also showed Senator Rubio was in fourth place in Iowa, but with 13% support.[30] For the New Hampshire primary, which is the second contest in the nation, a Fox News poll published on November 18th, 2015 showed Senator Rubio with 13% support,

---

[27] The Editorial Board. "Time for Other GOP Candidates to Call Out Trump." *San Diego Union-Tribune.* November 24th, 2015.
[28] Gass, Nick. "Rep. Issa Throws His Support Behind Rubio." Politico. November 30th, 2015.
[29] Salvanto, Anthony; De Pinto, Jen; Dutton, Sarah; and Backus, Fred. "Poll: Trump retakes lead, Cruz surges in IA; Rubio Second in NH." CBS News. November 22nd, 2015.
[30] Quinnipiac University Poll: "Trump, Cruz On Top In Topsy-Turvy Iowa GOP Caucus, Quinnipiac University Poll Finds; Keep Syrian Refugees Out, Republicans Say 5-1." November 24th, 2015.

in second place behind Donald Trump.[31]   A CBS News poll published four days later showed the same results.[32]

In December, an editorial in the *San Diego Union-Tribune* asked: "Can't anyone derail the Trump train?"   Donald Trump's "confident, relatively restrained performance" in the most recent debate had caused "non-xenophobes" to pray that the candidate would exit the race after losing in early primary states. The alternative, the Editorial Board claimed, is depression. The editorial ended with the statement: "It is a sad comment on the times that Trump's enduring popularity requires taking his candidacy seriously."[33]

Another editorial, later that month, criticized Senator Rubio for placing a hold on the nomination of Assistant Secretary of State Roberta Jacobson to the post of U.S. ambassador to Mexico, which had already been approved by the Republican-controlled Senate Foreign Relations Committee. His main reason for doing so was her involvement in the

---

[31] Fox News Poll: "Trump, Sanders lead respective primaries in New Hampshire." November 18th, 2015.

[32] Salvanto, Anthony; De Pinto, Jen; Dutton, Sarah; and Backus, Fred. "Poll: Trump retakes lead, Cruz surges in IA; Rubio Second in NH." CBS News. November 22nd, 2015.

[33] The Editorial Board. "Can't Anyone Derail the Trump Train?" *San Diego Union-Tribune.* December 17th, 2015.

normalization of relations with Cuba, which Senator Rubio opposed. The Editorial Board claimed this action was "a political misstep that hurts the United States."[34]

By the end of 2015, Issa for Congress had raised $530,000, spent $477,000, and had $3.8 million cash on hand.[35] The campaign, again, spent the largest proportion of its expenses on fundraising and media consulting services. These services cost $47,000 over the three months.[36] Applegate for Congress, in contrast, had only spent $10,400 on compliance services, $7,100 on information technology, $5,693.34 on rent, and a minimal amount on credit card processing fees and printing.[37]

Because the 2016 general election was also a presidential election, we can use the candidates' views as a proxy for the views of their respective political parties. What does a voter that identifies with the Republican Party generally believe compared to a voter that identifies with the Democratic Party? Each presidential candidate lays out his or her worldview and priorities in an

---

[34] The Editorial Board. "Marco Rubio's Ambassadorial Misstep." *San Diego Union-Tribune.* December 30th, 2015.

[35] Filing FEC-1045748. Form 3: Year-End. Filed January 29th, 2016.

[36] Filing FEC-1045748. Schedule B. Filed January 29th, 2016.

[37] Filing FEC-1046515. Schedule B. Filed January 31st, 2016.

announcement speech. Among Republican Party candidates, Senator Cruz, Senator Rubio, and Donald Trump's announcement speeches will be compared to understand the worldview and priorities of their supporters. These candidates are more relevant to the 49th Congressional District than other candidates because Congressman Issa endorsed Senator Rubio, Senator Cruz hired national campaign staff from the San Diego County Republican Party and campaigned near the district, and Donald Trump was the eventual nominee. Among Democratic Party candidates, Secretary Clinton and Senator Sanders' announcement speeches will be compared to understand the worldview and priorities of their supporters. These candidates are more relevant to the 49th Congressional District than other candidates because they were the only candidates still in the race by the June 7th, 2016 primary in California.

Senator Cruz asked: "What is the promise of America?" His answer: "The idea—the revolutionary idea—that this country was founded upon, which is that our rights do not come from man. They come from God Almighty."

A reference was made to American exceptionalism, which Senator Cruz claimed "made this nation a clarion voice for freedom in the world, a shining city on a hill," and "makes this nation an indispensable nation, a unique nation in the history of the world."

The first group Senator Cruz appealed to were Christians. He claimed roughly half of born-again Christians were not voting, but asked the audience to "Imagine instead millions of people of faith all across America coming out to the polls and voting our values."

As Senator Cruz began to describe the desired end goals of a Cruz presidency, we see the candidate's preferences. Without going into the means to an end, he listed booming economic growth, thriving innovation on the Internet, and energy self-sufficiency as his first three desired end-goals. In terms of specific policy, he advocated repealing Obamacare in order to make "health insurance personal and portable and affordable." He also advocated abolishing the Internal Revenue Service. Only after mentioning these issues, did Senator Cruz bring up immigration. Yet, all he asked the audience to do was "imagine a legal immigration system that welcomes and celebrates those who come to achieve the American dream."

In Senator Cruz's eyes, the federal government was waging an assault on religious liberty, undermining the right to bear arms, and spying on Americans. Instead, he wanted a federal government that "works to defend the sanctity of human life and to uphold the sacrament of marriage." Referring to the Second and Fourth Amendment, he asked the audience to "imagine a federal government that protects the right to keep and bear arms of all law-abiding Americans," and "protected the privacy rights of every American." He advocated abolishing Common Core and called school choice "the civil rights issue of the next generation."

On foreign policy, Senator Cruz criticized President Obama for boycotting Israeli Prime Minister Benjamin Netanyahu, end-running Congress by going to the United Nations to deal with Iran, and refusing to call radical Islamic terrorism by its name.

Senator Cruz conceded that "all of these seem difficult, indeed to some they may seem unimaginable." He then referred back to daunting periods in American history. In 1775, Patrick Henry said, "Give me liberty or give me death." In 1776, the 56 signers of the Declaration of Independence pledged their lives, their fortunes, and their sacred honor. In 1777, General Washington was losing battle after battle against the most powerful army in the world. In 1933, President Roosevelt faced crushing depression at home and gathering storms abroad. In 1979, America faced crushing stagnation at home and a hostage crisis and a Cold War abroad. In Senator

Cruz's words, "From the dawn of this country, at every stage America has enjoyed God's providential blessing. Over and over again, when we face impossible odds, the American people rose to the challenge."

Senator Cruz referred to his base as "courageous conservatives" and asked them to "come together to reclaim the promise of America, to reclaim the mandate, the hope and opportunity for our children and our children's children."

"The answer," claimed Senator Cruz, "will not come from Washington." Instead, "It will only come as it has come at every other time of challenge in this country, when the American people stand together and say we will get back to the principles that have made this country great." Senator Cruz then ended his speech with: "We will get back and restore that shining city on a hill that is the United States of America."

The "Imagine Speech" was less than 2,500 words. The first 1,000 words discussed Senator Cruz's parents, his upbringing, and his wife. The remaining 1,500 words were focused on ideology and policy. Cruz conservatism appealed heavily to religious faith, specifically Christianity. God was mentioned multiple times. The speech was made at

Liberty University, which Senator Cruz called "the largest Christian university in the world."

One common theme throughout the speech was the belief that the federal government is an obstacle to progress, not a driver of progress. The employment issue was mentioned multiple times, but foreign trade was not. Senator Cruz did not seek to alter the source or level of inbound immigration, instead he referred to America as "the one land on earth that has welcomed so many millions," and sought to have a system that welcomes and celebrates more legal immigration. Besides Israel and Iran, Senator Cruz did not mention America's relationships with other countries.

Senator Rubio gave his announcement speech at Freedom Tower, in Miami, Florida. He chose the location because it is a symbol of America's "identity as a land of opportunity." America was different from other countries because Americans are the children and grandchildren of people who refused to accept "the circumstances of their birth."

The problem Senator Rubio saw was that "now too many Americans are starting to doubt whether achieving that dream is still possible." In his words, it was "because while our people and our economy are pushing the boundaries of the 21st century, too many of our leaders and their ideas are stuck in the 20th century."

Senator Rubio focused first on employment. He criticized America's leaders for "taxing and borrowing and regulating like it was 1999," and also stated they "blindly support an outdated higher education system that is too expensive and too inaccessible to those who need it most." In foreign affairs, America's leaders "have forgotten when America fails to lead, global chaos inevitably follows."

Senator Rubio then stated his priorities and path to a new American century. He called for tax reform, without mentioning which direction tax rates would go. He called for fewer regulations without going into specifics. He stated he would control spending, but did not indicate whether that meant smaller spending increases than otherwise or a balanced budget. He wanted immigration laws to be "modernized," but did not specify how that would change the sources or level of immigration. Lastly, he called for repealing and replacing Obamacare. The end result of these actions, in Senator Rubio's words, would be "millions of better-paying modern jobs."

In terms of social issues, Senator Rubio asked the audience to remember "the family, not the government, is the most important institution in our society," and to remember "all human life deserves protection of our laws." Senator Rubio mentioned God multiple times, and quoted the Bible.

On foreign relations, Senator Rubio claimed he would reverse the Obama administration's "dangerous concessions to Iran and its hostility to Israel." Accepting the mantle of global leadership meant "no long being passive in the face of Chinese and Russian aggression," and "ending the near total disregard for the erosion of democracy and human rights around the world, especially Cuba, Venezuela, and Nicaragua."

Senator Rubio saw the 2016 election as "a generational choice about what kind of country we will be." He described Hillary Clinton as "a leader from yesterday," that "began a campaign for president by promising to take us back to yesterday." He called on Americans to "change the decisions we are making by changing the people who are making them."

Senator Cruz and Senator Rubio's speeches build an outline of Republican Party principles leading up to the 2016 election. Both candidates focused on religious faith. Both viewed the United States as a unique country because it provides opportunities to its people like no other country. Both sought a reduced role for the federal government, especially related to healthcare. Both candidates were friendly to Israel and hostile to Iran, but Senator Rubio went further in calling for active responses against China, Russia, Cuba, Venezuela, and Nicaragua.

In terms of priorities, both candidates put tax and regulation issues ahead of immigration issues. Neither candidate indicated they desired reduced immigration, and Senator Rubio even said a sentence in Spanish. Neither candidate criticized America's military alliances or trade deals with other countries. To them, America is a nation within the global economy. They do not see America as a nation with an economy. Neither candidate mentioned crime.

Donald Trump, by comparison, began the policy portion of his speech with the sentence: "Our country is in serious trouble." He asked the audience: "When was the last time anybody saw us beating, let's say, China in a trade deal? ... When did we beat Japan at anything? ... When do we beat Mexico at the border?"

Although America of the past might have been "a shining city on a hill" or had an "identity as a land of opportunity" to use Senator Cruz and Senator Rubio's words, but now, in Donald Trump's view, "The U.S. has become a dumping ground for everybody else's problems."

Senator Cruz and Senator Rubio did not mention Mexico in their speeches, but Donald Trump claimed, "When Mexico sends its people, they're not sending their best. ... They're bringing drugs. They're bringing crime. They're rapists. And some, I assume, are good people." While Senator Rubio mentioned the erosion of democracy and human rights in Cuba, Venezuela, and Nicaragua, Donald Trump focused on those nation's impact on American livelihood. The problems at the border were "coming from all over South and Latin America, and its coming probably—probably—from the Middle East."

Next, Donald Trump spoke about the economy. He referenced the labor participation rate, which was the worst it had been since 1978. He referenced the gross domestic product growth rate, which was below zero. He also stated: "Our real unemployment is anywhere from 18 to 20 percent. Don't believe the 5.6 percent."

Much of Donald Trump's speech referred to his business success, personal wealth, and stories from his relationships with political and business leaders. According to Corey Lewandowski, the campaign manager of the Trump campaign at that time, the original speech was supposed to be seven-

and-a-half minutes. Instead, it turned into "a forty-five-minute freestyle soliloquy."[38]

At the end of the speech, Donald Trump listed the things he would do as president. First, he would repeal and replace Obamacare, which he called "the big lie." Next, he would build a wall on the U.S. southern border, and "have Mexico pay for that wall." He promised to stop Iran from getting nuclear weapons. On immigration policy, he would "immediately terminate President Obama's illegal executive order." He would "Fully support and back up the Second Amendment" and end Common Core. Without going into specifics, he claimed he would rebuild America's infrastructure, "save Medicare, Medicaid, and Social Security without cuts," renegotiate trade deals, and reduce America's $18 trillion national debt. He ended the speech by declaring: "Sadly, the American dream is dead," but promised he would "bring it back bigger and better and stronger than ever before, and we will make America great again!"

Senator Sanders launched his candidacy for president to "begin a political revolution to transform our country economically, politically, socially, and

---

[38] Lewandowski, Corey and Bossie, David. "Let Trump be Trump." Published by Center Street, a division of Hachette Book Group, Inc. 2017. Page 82-83.

environmentally." America was to be, once again, "the leader in the world in the fight for economic and social justice, for environmental sanity and for a world of peace." He gave the speech along the shore of Lake Champlain, in Vermont. While mayor of Burlington, he converted the waterfront from "an unsightly rail yard that served no public purpose and was an eyesore," into a "beautiful people-oriented public space."

In Senator Sanders' view, America "faces more serious problems today than at any time since the Great Depression and, if you include the planetary crisis of climate change, it may well be that the challenges we face now are direr than any time in our modern history."

Wealth and income inequality "is the great moral issue of our time, it is the great economic issue of our time and it is the great political issue of our time." On the issue of employment, Senator Sanders stated: "The truth is that real unemployment is not the 5.4 percent you read in the newspapers. It is close to 11 percent if you include those workers who have given up looking for jobs or who are working part time when they want to work full time." As a result of the Supreme Court's *Citizens United* decision, Senator Sanders claimed, "the American political system has been totally corrupted, and the foundations of American democracy are being undermined." In terms of climate change, Senator Sanders stated: "It is caused by human activity and it is already causing devastating problems in the United States and around the world."

Senator Sanders then provided a vision of a very different America. He called for a $1 trillion infrastructure plan over five years, an end to trade policies as they currently exist, a multi-year increase in the federal minimum wage from $7.25 to $15 an hour, revised overtime rules, guaranteed paid leave, "a tax system which is fair and progressive, which makes wealthy individuals and profitable corporations begin to pay their fair share of taxes," an end to "too big to fail" financial regulations, a constitutional amendment to overturn *Citizens United*, public funding of elections, a tax on carbon "to accelerate the transition away from fossil fuel," a Medicare-for-All single-payer system, expanded Social Security benefits, a universal pre-K system, tuition-free public colleges and universities, lower interest rates on student loans, and a Muslim-led international coalition to defeat the Islamic State of Iraq and Syria (ISIS). Senator Sanders did mention "pay equity for women workers" and African-American youth unemployment being higher than the overall unemployment rate. Gender and racial issues were presented in economic terms, except for Senator Sanders' desire to live in a country "Where every person, no matter their race, their religion, their disability or their sexual orientation realizes the full promise of equality that is our birthright as Americans."

Senator Sanders did not mention President Obama specifically, despite seeking the nomination of his party to succeed him, and did not directly criticize Hillary Clinton. He criticized "presidents from both parties," which would include President Obama and President Clinton, for supporting "trade agreements which have cost us millions of decent paying jobs as corporate America shuts down plants here and moves to low-wage countries." Senator Sanders mentioned that he voted against the war in Iraq, and called it "the right vote," but did not allude to then-Senator Clinton's vote for the war.

Secretary Clinton made her announcement speech at the Franklin D. Roosevelt Four Freedoms Park in New York City. There were three aspects of the location that had symbolism for her campaign. First, the park was right across the water from the United Nations headquarters, where she represented the United States many times. Second, the park was dedicated to "Franklin Roosevelt's enduring vision of

America." Lastly, the location had "absolutely no ceilings," referring to the so-called "glass ceiling."

In Secretary Clinton's view, President Roosevelt's Four Freedoms are both a testament to America's "unmatched aspirations" and a reminder of the nation's "unfinished work at home and abroad." President Obama and President Clinton "were and are two Democrats guided by the fundamental American belief that real and lasting prosperity must be built by all and shared by all."

Under President Obama, America "pulled back from the brink of Depression, saved the auto industry, provided health care to 16 million working people, and replaced the jobs we lost faster than after a financial crash," but Secretary Clinton also conceded many Americans were still wondering "When does my hard work pay off? When does my family get ahead?"

When comparing herself with Republicans, Secretary Clinton began to highlight her priorities. She mentioned income inequality first. She then called climate change "one of the defining threats of our time." She claimed Republicans "want to take away health insurance from more than 16 million Americans without offering any credible alternative." Abortion was the next issue mentioned, in which Secretary Clinton stated Republicans "shame and blame women, rather than respect our right to make our own reproductive health decisions." She claimed she did not want to "put immigrants, who work hard and pay taxes, at risk of deportation." Lastly, she claimed Republicans "turn their backs on gay people who love each other." In summary, the goal and order of priorities was to reverse income inequality and climate change while maintaining the Affordable Care Act, abortion, amnesty, and gay marriage.

Secretary Clinton promised to "wage and win" the Four Fights. The first fight was "to make the economy work for everyday Americans, not just those at the top." The second fight was "to strengthen America's families, because when our families are strong, America is strong." The third fight was "to harness all of America's power, smarts, and values to maintain our leadership for peace, security, and prosperity." The fourth fight was "reforming our government and revitalizing our democracy so that it works for everyday Americans."

Overseas, Russia, North Korea, and Iran were "traditional threats." America also had "to deal with the rise of new powers like China." In her role as Secretary of State, she "stood up to adversaries like Putin and reinforced allies like Israel." In Secretary Clinton's determination, "No other country is better prepared to meet emerging threats from cyber attacks, transnational terror networks like ISIS, and diseases that spread across oceans and continents."

Senator Sanders and Secretary Clinton's speeches build an outline of Democratic Party principles leading up to the 2016 election. Secretary Clinton made her announcement speech after Senator Sanders, which might be the reason income inequality was the first issue for both candidates. Both candidates viewed the United States as a leader in global initiatives. Senator Sanders focused global issues almost exclusively in terms of stopping climate change, whereas Secretary Clinton expanded that role to include security affairs. Both candidates desired a significant increase in the size and scope of the federal government, although Secretary Clinton often mentioned private sector initiatives along with government programs. Secretary Clinton advocated amnesty for illegal immigrants and defended abortion, whereas Senator Sanders did not mention either issue. Neither candidate mentioned the national debt.

Contrasting the five candidates' worldview and policy prescriptions provides a glimpse into the priorities of each candidate's supporters. As these candidates advanced through the general, we can also get a sense for how their appeal will drive voters to participate in the 49th Congressional District election.

CHAPTER 3: THE NEW YEAR

The California Secretary of State published voter registration statistics by congressional district on January 5th, 2016. Since the previous report, total registrations had declined by more than 18,000 voters in the 49th Congressional District. The Republican registration advantage declined from 40,000 to 36,000 voters. Although both parties saw declines in voter registrations, about 8,000 fewer voters identified with the Republican Party (or left the district), whereas only about 4,000 fewer voters identified with the Democratic Party (or left the district).

South Carolina Governor Nikki Haley gave the Republican response to President Obama's State of the Union address. As part of her response, she denounced the "angriest voices," referring to Donald Trump. An editorial in the *San Diego Union-Tribune* highlighted the criticisms Governor Haley had received for her statements toward Donald Trump from radio host Rush Limbaugh and Congressman Steve King, a Republican from Iowa. The Editorial Board believed the Republican Party wanted "to cultivate a more tolerant image for their party," but also "to benefit from the populist backlash that is driving Trump's popularity." The Editorial Board believed reconciling those two goals was impossible.[39]

The last Republican debate before the Iowa caucuses was hosted by Fox News, in Des Moines, on January 28th, 2016. It was the seventh debate for Republican candidates this election. Donald Trump did not attend the debate. During the debate, three video clips were shown of Senator Rubio stating he opposes amnesty for illegal aliens, yet he later co-sponsored the Border Security, Economic Opportunity, and Immigration Modernization Act in 2013, which would have granted citizenship to illegal aliens. The four Democrat senators and four Republican senators that co-sponsored the bill became known as the "Gang of Eight." Senator Rubio stumbled in explaining the inconsistencies. The next day, during an interview with the *Boston Herald*,

---

[39] The Editorial Board. "'Principled Conservative' = Immigrant Basher?" *San Diego Union-Tribune.* January 15th, 2016.

Congressman Issa admitted he was "less than thrilled when [Senator Rubio] was part of the Gang of Eight," but claimed Senator Rubio was strong in the previous debate because he was able to explain his evolution.[40]

The Republican caucus in Iowa was held on February 1st, 2016. Senator Cruz came in first place, with 51,666 votes and 27.64% of the vote. Senator Rubio came in third place, with 43,228 votes and 23.12% of the vote. He picked up seven of 30 delegates. An editorial in the *Orange County Register* attempted to categorize each candidate as establishment or anti-establishment. On the Democrat side, the split was relatively easy between former Secretary of State Hillary Clinton and self-described democratic socialist Senator Sanders. On the Republican side, the determination was more difficult. The editorial categorized Senator Rubio, former Florida Governor Jeb Bush, New Jersey Governor Chris Christie, and Ohio Governor John Kasich as establishment candidates. Combined, those candidates received 23.1% of the vote in the Iowa caucus. The anti-establishment candidates were Senator Cruz, Senator Paul, Donald Trump, Dr. Ben Carson, and Carly Fiorina. Combined, those

---

[40] Chabot, Hillary. "Cruz Camp Admits Candidate Stung by Fox Debate Moderators." *Boston Herald*. January 30th, 2016.

candidates received 67.7% of the vote.[41] Clearly, there was a desire among caucus-goers to nominate an anti-establishment candidate.

A Republican debate was held on February 6th, 2016. Senator Rubio was criticized for being a one-term senator trying to run for president, just like President Obama did in 2008. In his response, he made the comment: "Let's dispel once and for all with this fiction that Barack Obama does not know what he is doing. He knows exactly what he is doing."

New Jersey Governor Chris Christie replied to Senator Rubio: "You have not been involved in a consequential decision where you had to be held accountable."

In his response to Governor Christie, Senator Rubio again used the line: "Let's dispel with this fiction that Barack Obama does not know what he is doing."

Governor Christie stated: "When you are president of the United States, when you are a governor of a state, the memorized 30-second speech where you talk about how great America is at the end of it does not solve one problem for one person."

---

[41] The Editorial Board. "Establishment stumbles out of the gate in Iowa." *Orange County Register*. February 3rd, 2016.

Senator Rubio's response—again—had the line: "This notion that Barack Obama does not know what he is doing is just not true."

Governor Christie cut in—immediately—to say: "There it is. There it is. The memorized, 25-second speech. There it is, everybody."

Senator Rubio again gave a response that included the line: "We are not facing a president that does not know what he is doing. He knows what he is doing." This brought into question his status as a potential front-runner.

The Republican primary in New Hampshire was held on February 9th, 2016. Donald Trump came in first place, with 100,735 votes and 35.23% of the vote. Senator Rubio came in fifth place, with 30,071 votes and 10.52% of the vote.[42] So far Senator Rubio had won nine delegates.

In response to Senator Sanders and Donald Trump's victory in the New Hampshire primary, the *Orange County Register* Editorial Board lamented: "We wish the candidates more emphasized freedom."[43]

---

[42] New Hampshire Secretary of State. 2016 Presidential Primary – Republican President.

[43] The Editorial Board. "This Revolution is Being Televised." *Orange County Register*. February 10th, 2016.

The Editorial Board of the *San Diego Union-Tribune* attempted to explain the success of Senator Sanders and Donald Trump. Senator Sanders' popularity was not driven by "fantasies peddled to people who want to be given things by government." Instead, he "shares the view of most liberals that not only were Wall Street machinations responsible for the Great Recession, but that tax, fiscal and regulatory policies coming out of Washington are intended to produce income inequality." Donald Trump's popularity was not driven by "nativism and lazy nationalism," although the Editorial Board claimed they were "major factors." Instead, his approach is "far more in tune with the Republican rank-and-file than the GOP senators who embrace comprehensive immigration reform." The Editorial Board called on "responsible leaders" of both parties to "figure this out before a bomb thrower moves into 1600 Pennsylvania Avenue."[44]

One week later, Congressman Issa appeared on CNN to discuss Senator Rubio's results in both the Iowa caucuses and the New Hampshire primary. Congressman Issa blamed Senator Rubio's poor performance in the debates on getting "caught in a

---

[44] The Editorial Board. "Why Bomb Throwers Sanders and Trump are Winning." *San Diego Union-Tribune.* February 12th, 2016.

trap by the relentless attack of the career prosecutor who has now left the race," referring to Governor Christie. He then attacked Donald Trump for hosting Hillary Clinton at his wedding and his criticisms of former Republican President George W. Bush's foreign policy.[45]

On February 13th, the 2016 U.S. presidential election became not just a contest to control the White House, but also the United States Supreme Court. Justice Scalia, a consistently conservative voice on the Supreme Court for three decades, was found dead at a resort in West Texas.[46]

Iowa Senator Charles Grassley, a Republican and Chairman of the Senate Judiciary Committee, said: "Given the huge divide in the country, and the fact that this president, above all others, has made no bones about his goal to use the courts to circumvent Congress and push through his own agenda, it only makes sense that we defer." The Editorial Board of the *San Diego Union-Tribune* labeled these calls to delay Scalia's replacement "corrosive," and said they had the effect of "predictably widening the country's deep partisan divide." The Editorial Board claimed:

---

[45] CNN: Legal View with Ashleigh Banfield. Aired 12:30-01:00PM EST, February 16th, 2016.

[46] Liptak, Adam. "Antonin Scalia, Justice on the Supreme Court, Dies at 79." *New York Times*. February 14th, 2016.

"To leave his seat vacant is to insult him and America."[47]

A few days later, the *San Diego Union-Tribune* Editorial Board lamented Justice Scalia had been embalmed the day after he was discovered dead, instead of performing an autopsy, based on the wishes of his family. The primary concern was this decision would spawn conspiracy theories. It used the opportunity to refer to Donald Trump as "the civic arsonist who is leading the Republican presidential race."[48]

The *San Diego Union-Tribune* ran a third editorial in February related to Justice Scalia's passing. In it, the Editorial Board pointed out that Senator Edward Kennedy, a Massachusetts Democrat, had denounced Judge Robert Bork from the Senate floor within the hour of President Reagan's nomination. Both Senator Obama and Senator Clinton had voted to support the filibuster of Judge Samuel Alito, who was President George W. Bush's nominee. Senator Reid, a Nevada Democrat, had repeatedly delayed or blocked Bush's judicial

---

[47] The Editorial Board. "Leaving Justice Scalia's Seat Vacant Insults Him, America." *San Diego Union-Tribune.* February 14th, 2016.

[48] The Editorial Board. "Scalia Should Have Had an Autopsy." *San Diego Union-Tribune.* February 18th, 2016.

nominations. However, the Editorial Board asserted, "Senate Majority Leader Mitch McConnell, R-Ky., has been far more aggressive toward the Obama White House, with only one federal appeals court nominee being confirmed in 2015." The Editorial Board conceded that Republican Party purity tests have led to electoral success, considering the party had captured the House in 2010 and the Senate in 2014, but also bemoaned that these same purity tests have had a negative effect on how Washington works. The editorial ended with the statement: "To the detriment of the nation, too many Republicans see that as a plus."[49]

The Republican primary in South Carolina was held on February 20th, 2016. Congressman Issa campaigned for Senator Rubio on February 17th and 18th. Senator Rubio came in second place, but because the contest was winner-takes-all, Donald Trump won all 50 delegates.

That same day, the *Orange County Register* reported that Irvine, the third largest city in Orange County, now had more registered Democrats than registered Republicans. Professor Jodi Balma of Fullerton College attributed the partisan shift to

---

[49] The Editorial Board. "Republican 'Tent' Keeps Getting Smaller." *San Diego Union-Tribune*. February 20th, 2016.

"Republicans becoming independents and independents moving in who might have registered as Republicans in the past." Henry Vandermeir, the chairman of the Democratic Party of Orange County, believed rhetoric by Republican presidential candidates was causing the shift, and was quoted by the newspaper as saying, "The GOP has helped us." Fred Whitaker, the chairman of the Republican Party of Orange County, acknowledged the decline, but claimed the party was more successful in local races in recent years.[50]

The Republican caucus in Nevada was held on February 23rd, 2016. That morning, Congressman Issa appeared on CNN. First, he re-iterated his reasons for supporting Senator Rubio by saying "This is somebody that I watched from the day he got here do two things: One, make a conservative approach to legislation and to oversight; and, two, reach out to all the parties in both the Republican Party and the Democratic Party." Then, he began bashing Donald Trump, noting that he invited Hillary Clinton to his wedding, but not Congressman Issa or Senator Rubio. Congressman Issa also questioned whether or not Donald Trump was a Republican. He then compared

---

[50] Wisckol, Martin. "Irvine is Latest Orange County City to Tilt Democratic." *Orange County Register*. February 20th, 2016.

Donald Trump to Todd Akin.[51] In the 2012 U.S. Senate election in Missouri, the *St. Louis Post-Dispatch* had found that three potential Republican candidates led in the polls against the Democrat incumbent Senator Claire McCaskill.[52] In the Republican primary election on August 7th, 2012, Congressman Akin came in first place with only 36.05% of the vote.[53] Less than two weeks later, during a televised interview on a local station, he responded to a question about abortion, in part, with the statement: "If it is a legitimate rape, the female body has ways to try to shut that whole thing down."[54] He lost the November election with only 39.11% of the vote, despite Republican presidential candidate Mitt Romney receiving 53.76% of the vote in Missouri.[55] Congressman Issa used this example to call on the majority of Republicans that had not indicated

---

[51] CNN: New Day with Chris Cuomo. Aired 08:30-09:00AM EST on February 23rd, 2016.

[52] McDermott, Kevin. "Claire McCaskill Trails GOP Candidates in Senate Race, Poll Shows." *St. Louis Post-Dispatch*. July 28th, 2012.

[53] Missouri Secretary of State. Primary Election – August 7th, 2012.

[54] Eligon, John; and Schwirtz, Michael. "Senate Candidate Provokes Ire With 'Legitimate Rape' Comment." *New York Times*. August 19th, 2012.

[55] Missouri Secretary of State. General Election – November 6th, 2012.

Donald Trump was their first choice, "to vote for the most conservative candidate that can win." For Congressman Issa, that was Senator Rubio.

Donald Trump would go on to win the Nevada Republican caucus, with 45.75% of the vote and 34,531 votes. Senator Rubio came in second place with 23.77% and 17,940 votes. Donald Trump had won more votes than all candidates in the 2012 Nevada Republican caucus combined, and Senator Rubio received more votes than Mitt Romney.[56] Senator Rubio had 16 delegates so far, behind both Donald Trump with 82 delegates and Senator Cruz with 17 delegates.

One day after Donald Trump's landslide victory in the Nevada Republican caucus, two Republican congressmen endorsed the candidate. One of them was San Diego County's own Congressman Duncan Hunter, who stated he had not spoken to the candidate before making the endorsement.[57]

Donald Trump's victories in the early primary states, followed by Congressman Duncan Hunter's endorsement, caused the *San Diego Union-Tribune*

---

[56] Nevada Secretary of State general election data.

[57] Stewart, Joshua. "Rep. Hunter Among First House Members to Endorse Trump." *San Diego Union-Tribune*. February 24th, 2016.

Editorial Board to revise its prior belief that the Republican candidate could not possibly win. The newspaper claimed it was mortified by the thought of President Trump, citing "casual cruelty, dishonesty and belligerence, his awful remarks about Mexicans and women, his ignorance about military and foreign policy issues, his open admiration for Russian dictator Vladimir Putin." The millions of Americans that support him, though, "believe that Trump grasps their problems and fears in ways the nation's leaders do not." The Editorial Board acknowledged attacks on Donald Trump by the media and conventional politicians of both parties made him even more attractive to certain voters. "The former secretary of state, New York senator and first lady," in contrast, "is a symbol of the political establishment at a time when many voters will see that as a negative." As before, the Editorial Board hoped that Donald Trump self-destructs.[58]

The Editorial Board of the *San Diego Union-Tribune* began to revisit its favorable opinion of Senator Rubio. Earlier that week, Senator Rubio had suggested at a campaign rally that Donald Trump had wet his pants on stage during a debate. Two days

---

[58] The Editorial Board. "Stop Saying Donald Trump Can't Win." *San Diego Union-Tribune.* February 26th, 2016.

later, he asked the crowd, "Have you seen his hands? You know what they say about men with small hands. You can't trust them." The Editorial Board accused Senator Rubio and Donald Trump of turning the election into the 2006 film "Idiocracy."[59]

On Super Tuesday, Donald Trump won seven states, Senator Cruz won two states (including his home state of Texas), and Senator Rubio won Minnesota. Hillary Clinton won seven states and Senator Sanders won four. An editorial in the *Orange County Register* reminded readers "Typically, the candidate that wins the most states on Super Tuesday goes on to win their party's nomination for the presidency."[60]

"Never before have we seen a major party's two previous presidential nominees renounce the current frontrunner," declared the *San Diego Union-Tribune* Editorial Board in response to Mitt Romney and John McCain's attacks on Donald Trump. The Editorial Board again claimed "bigotry and raw nativism" were the main drivers of Donald Trump's appeal, but also stated, "part of it is built on the vast

---

[59] The Editorial Board. "Trump, Rubio Turn Presidential Campaign into 'Idiocracy.'" *San Diego Union-Tribune.* February 29th, 2016.

[60] The Editorial Board. "Trump Triumphs; Clinton Douses 'Bern.'" *Orange County Register*. March 2nd, 2016.

alienation that millions of people feel because life doesn't seem to be getting better for the middle class and poor people in America." The Editorial Board seemed to admit that failure to acknowledge or address these issues made Donald Trump more appealing to the disaffected when he is attacked by establishment political leaders like Mitt Romney, John McCain, and Hillary Clinton.[61]

On March 4th, 2016, Congressman Issa again went on CNN to defend Senator Rubio and attack Donald Trump. In response to Donald Trump reversing his view on torture, Congressman Issa said, "I think it is an example of somebody who is not ready to be the commander in chief." He also claimed Donald Trump was "a man who mocked and said unconscionable things about John McCain." Congressman Issa answered in the affirmative when asked whether he was concerned for the safety of the country should Donald Trump become president. He stated he would not vote for Hillary Clinton, but he was unwilling to commit to vote for Donald Trump.[62]

---

[61] The Editorial Board. "Donald Trump, Great Power and Greater Irresponsibility." *San Diego Union-Tribune.* March 3rd, 2016.

[62] CNN: The Situation Room with Wolf Blitzer. Aired 06:00-07:00PM EST on March 4th, 2016.

Former First Lady Nancy Reagan passed away in early March, 2016. The *San Diego Union-Tribune* Editorial Board described the modern Republican Party's reverence for President Reagan "both ironic and a cause for melancholy." In terms of outlook, the Editorial Board compared "Reagan and his optimism about America's best days being ahead" with Donald Trump and Senator Cruz, who "depict an America in rapid decline and view consensus ominously."[63]

After losing the winner-takes-all primary in his home state of Florida, Senator Rubio suspended his campaign on March 15th, 2016.[64] Congressman Issa's first choice was out of the race. The *San Diego Union-Tribune* Editorial Board told its readers to "brace yourselves," because California "may very well decide whether Donald Trump is the Republican nominee." The Editorial Board seemed to be cheering for Senator Cruz, after acknowledging that Governor Kasich needed "a mathematically impossible 112 percent of the remaining delegates to win the

---

[63] The Editorial Board. "Ronald, Nancy Reagan Rose from a Different GOP." *San Diego Union-Tribune.* March 7th, 2016.
[64] Peters, Jeremy; and Barbaro, Michael. "A Distant Second at Home, Marco Rubio Ends a Disappointing Campaign." *New York Times.* March 15th, 2016.

nomination on a first ballot at the Republican convention."[65]

Senator Sanders launched the contest for California's delegates on March 22nd, 2016. More than 10,000 supporters waited for hours to hear him speak during a late-night rally at the San Diego Convention Center.[66]

The San Diego County Republican Party held its 2016 Lincoln Reagan Dinner at the Hilton Bayfront on Monday, March 28th. Utah Senator Mike Lee was the keynote speaker. According to the chairman of the party, attendance had increased every year for at least five years, and had outgrown other venues. There were 750 attendees in 2016 and the event raised over $405,000, up from over $350,000 the year before, through sponsorships and ticket sales.

During the event, Orange County teacher Rebecca Friedrichs received the Torch of Freedom award. Her lawsuit, *Friedrichs v. California Teachers Association*, argued that being compelled to pay union fees, which are used for political speech, violated her free speech rights. The Supreme Court heard the case on January 11th, but Justice Scalia's death on

---

[65] The Editorial Board. "California Primary Could Seal the Deal for Donald Trump." *San Diego Union-Tribune*. March 17th, 2016.
[66] Molnar, Phillip; Stewart, Joshua. "Sanders Revs Up Huge San Diego Crowd." *San Diego Union-Tribune*. March 23rd, 2016.

February 13th meant a tied vote would allow the lower court's decision to stand.[67] In fact, the day after the event in San Diego, the Supreme Court affirmed the lower court's judgment by an equally divided court.[68]

In March, the *San Diego Union-Tribune* published two editorials related to the Supreme Court. In the first, the Editorial Board speculated whether or not there would be seven Supreme Court justices before there were nine. The Editorial Board had hoped "independent and constructive" Republicans such as Senator Olympia Snowe, Senator Susan Collins, Senator John McCain, Senator Lisa Murkowski, and Senator Lindsey Graham would have voted with Democrat senators to confirm Merrick Garland, President Obama's nominee to the Supreme Court, but lamented "such a conventional execution of its duties seems beyond the obstructionist Senate." Despite the Editorial Board's dismay, it did acknowledge "Republicans understand something that others sometimes do not about the mood of the country: their near-reflexive opposition to Obama's policies and initiatives has propelled them to power unseen in years." The Editorial Board

---

[67] Stewart, Joshua. "County GOP Honors Teacher Challenging Union Fees." *San Diego Union-Tribune.* March 28th, 2016.
[68] *Friedrichs v. California Teachers Association*, 14-915.

expected the gridlock in the U.S. Senate would mean the ideological tie in the Supreme Court would only be broken once another justice steps down or dies. This was described as "a morbid Supreme Court death watch and a complete abdication of constitutional duty."[69] After the *Friedrichs v. California Teachers Association* decision was handed down, the *San Diego Union-Tribune*'s second editorial related to the Supreme Court called the case "a fresh reminder of the folly of Senate Republicans refusing to take up Judge Merrick Garland's nomination for the high court." Oddly, the Editorial Board tried to convince Republicans that a left-leaning justice should be placed on the Supreme Court in order to resolve pending cases involving abortion and affirmative action.[70]

Justice Scalia's successor would be appointed by the president and confirmed by the U.S. Senate, but California Republicans had a negligible impact on either contest. It was very unlikely Donald Trump would win California's 55 winner-takes-all electoral votes, no matter how many California Republicans showed up to vote. The contest to elect California's

---

[69] The Editorial Board. "Will We See 7 Supreme Court Justices Before We See 9?" *San Diego Union-Tribune*. March 17th, 2016.
[70] The Editorial Board. "Tie Supreme Court Vote Illustrates Senate GOP's Folly." *San Diego Union-Tribune*. March 30th, 2016.

U.S. Senator was already expected to be a contest between two Democrats. The only positive impact California Republicans could have on the 2016 election was re-electing Republican House representatives. This dynamic would help Congressman Issa later on.

That Wednesday, Senator Cruz traveled to Los Angeles to appear on "Jimmy Kimmel Live." On Thursday morning, he met with about 100 potential delegates to the Republican National Convention at the Hotel Irvine, in Orange County. At midday, Senator Cruz held a $1,000-per-person campaign fundraiser in Newport Beach. The event was held at the Pacific Club and organized by Republican Congressman Rohrabacher. Senator Cruz noted "Orange County is tremendously important. It was the birthplace of the Reagan revolution." Congressman Rohrabacher called Senator Cruz "the Ronald Reagan of this generation." A dinner was also hosted at the Beverly Hills Hotel. The *Orange County Register* reported on the events, and noted "The latest USC Dornsife/Los Angeles Times poll shows that Trump continues to lead and had the support of 37 percent of the California GOP voters surveyed, up from 24 percent in September. Meanwhile, Cruz, who was in single digits in the fall poll, saw his support grow to 30 percent."[71]

The same dynamic that propelled Donald Trump's campaign in the rest of the country mirrored itself among California Republicans. As former and current Republican officials tried to stop Donald Trump from receiving the nomination, his support among rank-and-file Republicans and conservatives grew. In a *San Diego Union-Tribune* survey of San Diego County Republican candidates and officeholders, none of the fifteen respondents said Donald Trump was their preferred candidate. The *Orange County Register* interviewed three members of the "well-heeled" Orange County Lincoln Club. All three members preferred Senator Rubio to Donald Trump.[72] Even College Republican clubs experienced this. The chairman of the San Diego State University College Republicans and the treasurer of UC San Diego College Republicans were both quoted as saying disparaging things about Donald Trump.[73] Despite this, Donald Trump was the first choice

---

[71] Kopetman, Roxana. "Senator Ted Cruz Makes Stop in Newport Beach, Saying 'Orange County is Tremendously Important.'" *Orange County Register*. April 1st, 2016.
[72] Wisckol, Martin. "Among Orange County's Republicans, Trump is Trouble." *Orange County Register*. February 25th, 2016.
[73] Stewart, Joshua. "San Diego's Trump Dilemma." *San Diego Union-Tribune*. April 2nd, 2016.

among Republican voters statewide, as mentioned above.

By the end of the first quarter of 2016, Issa for Congress had raised $674,000, spent $637,000, and had $3.7 million cash on hand.[74] The campaign's largest expenses in the period were $36,000 for tax payments on interest earned, $30,000 for strategic consulting services, $25,000 for printing and mailing, $20,000 on fundraising consulting services, and $10,000 for donations to the Orange County and San Diego County Republican Parties.[75] Applegate for Congress had raised $50,000, spent $39,000, and had $10,000 cash on hand.[76]

On April 1st, the *San Diego Union-Tribune* Editorial Board pleaded with California Republicans to not hand the nomination to Donald Trump, telling them to "consider all the outrageous, hateful and strange things that Trump has said and done." The Editorial Board believed his national defense policy would cause a mutiny and his economic policy would cause a global recession. The Editorial Board called the candidate "proudly offensive and vindictive,

---

[74] Filing FEC-1063800. Form 3: April Quarterly. Filed April 15th, 2016.

[75] Filing FEC-1063800. Schedule B. Filed April 15th, 2016.

[76] Filing FEC-1151320. April Quarterly. Amendment 3. Filed March 3rd, 2017.

demonizing large segments of the population, forgiving the blatant racism and the violence of some supporters, mocking the handicaps of one journalist and suggesting another journalist's menstrual cycle affected her behavior, and insulting the physical appearance of his rivals and even their family members."   Ironically, while attempting to hold Donald Trump accountable for his behavior, the newspaper noted that, for his supporters, "attempts to hold him accountable for his appalling behavior only reinforce his appeal to them." To those people, the Editorial Board hoped "they step back and think about the fact that Trump may rebrand the GOP in his image for decades to come."[77] Four days later, the Editorial Board declared, "Trump's chances for the GOP nomination, much less to win the White House, seem to be fading by the day."[78]

The Sanders campaign released a press release praising legislation signed by Governor Jerry Brown of California and Governor Andrew Cuomo of New York to raise the minimum wage to $15 per hour over the next few years. The candidate stated: "As president, I will proudly stand with working families

---

[77] The Editorial Board. "For California and Trump, June 7 a Day of Reckoning." *San Diego Union-Tribune.* April 1st, 2016.
[78] The Editorial Board. "Trump's Border Wall Payment Plan in a Word? Cockamamie." *San Diego Union-Tribune.* April 5th, 2016.

all across our country and fight for Congress to raise the federal minimum wage to $15 an hour and provide paid family leave to every worker in America."[79]

The California Secretary of State provided an update of voter registration per congressional district on April 8th, 2016.[80] The Republican registration advantage decreased to 34,000 voters in the 49th Congressional District. Since the previous report, total Democrat voter registrations increased by 2,848 voters, while total Republican voter registrations only increased by 80 voters. Voters registered with other political parties or non-affiliated voters declined by over 3,000 voters. Nationally, the NBC News/Wall Street Journal Survey found 47% of respondents preferred a Democrat-controlled Congress in the upcoming election, whereas only 45% of respondents preferred a Republican-controlled Congress. The remaining 8% of respondents were undecided. Between April and the previous survey in October, the percent of respondents preferring a Republican-controlled Congress had not changed, but about 20%

---

[79] Bernie Sanders Campaign Press Release: "Sanders Statement on New York and California Minimum Wage Increase." April 4th, 2016.
[80] California Secretary of State. Report of Registration by Congressional District: April 8th, 2016.

of undecided respondents in October swung towards the Democrats by April. Two aspects of the survey stand out related to the 49th Congressional District. The survey found that 26% of respondents would be less likely to support a Republican candidate for Congress if Donald Trump as the Republican nominee for president. Only 21% of respondents would be less likely to support a Democrat candidate for Congress if Hillary Clinton was the Democrat nominee. Similar questions were not asked related to Senator Cruz or Senator Sanders.[81] That result did not bode well for Congressman Issa. When asked which party would be better at dealing with the ISIS, Republicans had a 19-point lead over Democrats. That result would likely favor the Republican candidate in a district that contains Camp Pendleton, which likely benefited Congressman Issa.

Senator Cruz returned to Orange County on April 11th, a Monday. He held a rally at the Hotel Irvine. According to tweets from the Orange County Republican Party, over 2,000 people attended the rally. The candidate later went to San Diego County for a rally at the Town and Country Resort in Mission Valley. "We are here tonight because our country is

---

[81] NBC News/Wall Street Journal Survey. Study #16229. Date Range: April 10th-14th, 2016.

in crisis, because we are bankrupting our kids and grandkids, because our constitutional rights are under assault, and because America has receded from leadership in the world," the candidate told the crowd. The rally coincided with the monthly meeting of the San Diego County Republican Party, so the candidate spoke directly to Republican Party activists with statements such as: "I am convinced the most long-lasting legacy of Barack Obama is going to be a new generation of leaders in the Republican Party who stand and fight for liberty, who stand and fight for the constitution, and who stand and fight for the Judeo-Christian values that built this great nation." According to a video statement posted on Twitter by the Chairman of the San Diego County Republican Party, over 3,000 people attended the rally, whereas only 300 people usually attend monthly meetings.

Both the Sanders campaign and Clinton campaign brought new voters to the Democratic Party in the places they visited in California, but their volunteer outreach was very different. "If the grass-roots campaigns in Orange County are any indication, Clinton's supporters learned little after losing to President Barack Obama's digital revolution two terms ago," reported the *Orange County Register*. During one weekend in April, about 40 Sanders supporters waved signs on the sidewalk to get drivers to honk to show their support for the candidate. By comparison, "a quiet collection of Hillary Clinton hopefuls sat in an Irvine cafe wondering what to call their group, wishing for a brick-and-mortar headquarters and asking who knew how to polish a Facebook page." At that point, the Sanders supporters' biggest concern was calling voters in New York to drive turnout for Senator Sanders in that state's primary. Clinton supporters worried "about bonding with Sanders supporters while presuming a Clinton win at the convention."[82]

The Sanders campaign released its first television ad in California on April 15th in San Francisco. The same ad was shown the next day in Los Angeles. The advertisement was titled "$27" which is a reference to the average contribution amount received by his campaign. By comparison, "Clinton is asking donors to raise $353,400 to get a seat next to her at the head table during two California fundraisers." In both cities, the ad was shown at approximately 8:00pm, "just as Secretary

---

[82] Whiting, David. "Bernie Sanders vs. Hillary Clinton: In Orange County, Their Supporters Take Different Approaches." *Orange County Register*. April 19th, 2016.

Clinton's wealthy donors are sitting down for dinner."[83]

Within three weeks of the *San Diego Union-Tribune* Editorial Board's determination that Trump's chances were fading by the day, another editorial was published to state their despair caused by the candidate's new momentum in the polls. The Editorial Board judged he was able to do this because Donald Trump "moderated his rhetoric and promoted the idea that long-established rules on how states picked delegates were 'rigged' against him by a desperate GOP establishment." The nomination of Donald Trump by one of America's two major parties was both "testament to how disaffected millions of Americans are," and "a testament to a cult-of-personality politics that is indistinguishable from mass superficiality." The Editorial Board welcomed the news that Senator Cruz and Senator Kasich would work together to deny Donald Trump the nomination. It also stated that Donald Trump would be a "down-ticket disaster" for the 24 Republican senators that were up for election that year.[84]

---

[83] Bernie Sanders Campaign Press Release: "Sanders Ad to Run Opposite Clinton Fundraiser." April 15th, 2016.

[84] The Editorial Board. "Ted Cruz, John Kasich vs. Donald Trump? Good!" *The San Diego Union-Tribune.* April 26th, 2016.

The Trump campaign held a rally in Costa Mesa on April 28th, 2016. Costa Mesa is in Orange County and less than 25 miles from the northern boundary of the 49th Congressional District. The *Orange County Register* reported "Hours before Republican presidential frontrunner Donald Trump was scheduled to make the first stop on his California campaign, large crowds of supporters and protesters were already gathering at the OC Fair and Event Center in Costa Mesa." It noted that the appeal of Orange County for the Trump campaign was the county's "longstanding national reputation as a Republican powerhouse." For other Republican candidates, the county's "many wealthy donors also make it a national fundraising hub." The speech was summarized as "short on policy specifics and long on emphasizing his campaign successes." However, at least 8,000 people showed up inside the Pacific Amphitheater to hear him make statements such as "No state has suffered more from open borders than the state of California."[85] After the rally, Donald Trump tweeted, "Thank you Costa Mesa, California!

---

[85] Wisckol, Martin; Haire, Chris; Schwebke, Scott; and Edwards Staggs, Brooke. "Donald Trump Rouses Cheering Crowd in Costa Mesa: 'Build that Wall.'" *Orange County Register*. April 29th, 2016.

31,000 people tonight with thousands turned away. I will be back!"

The next day, CBS Morning News included a television report on the anti-Trump protests the previous day in Costa Mesa. Correspondent Brook Silva-Braga reported "Anti-Donald Trump protesters clashed with police outside an amphitheater in Costa Mesa, California, late Thursday night. Some in the crowd held Dump Trump signs as they blocked traffic. Others took their frustrations out on a police car."[86] CBS This Morning correspondent Carter Evans reported "People yelled obscenities and held up signs protesting the Republican frontrunner. The crowd cheered on several people trying to flip over a vandalized police car. Others danced and waved Mexican flags, objecting to Trump's controversial immigration proposals." He also reported, "A man wearing a gray pro Trump T-shirt was seen with a bloodied face. He was treated by paramedics and loaded into an ambulance."[87]

The O'Reilly Factor showed clips of the violence in Costa Mesa from the previous night. Bill O'Reilly, the host, stated, "When Americans see people destroying police cars and generally behaving

---

[86] CBS Morning News. Aired April 29th, 2016.
[87] CBS This Morning. Aired April 29th, 2016.

in untoward way, they don't like those people." His historical example was Richard Nixon's campaign against George McGovern, and claimed, "The violent demonstrations against Nixon actually propelled him to a landslide victory even though the man himself was not generally liked." Mr. O'Reilly later said, "I will tell you what helps Trump the most. When you see these guys with the Mexican flags, waving the Mexican flags, that just takes people, independent people, who do not know about Trump one way or the other." In Mr. O'Reilly's assessment, the anti-Trump violence gave the candidate a three or four percent boost in the polls.[88] According to Adweek, Bill O'Reilly's show reached 2.2 million viewers that night, more than any other show on Fox News, CNN, or MSNBC.[89]

Footage of the violence was also shown on the Rachel Maddow Show, which is MSNBC's most popular show.[90] Rachel Maddow, the host, ended that portion of the segment with the statement: "Honestly, no matter how unfavorably somebody is

---

[88] Fox News: The O'Reilly Factor. Aired April 29th, 2016.

[89] Katz, A.J. "Scoreboard: Friday, April 29." Adweek.com. May 2nd, 2016.

[90] Katz, A.J. "Q1 2016 Ratings: MSNBC Regains Its Footing After Poor 2015." Adweek.com March 29th, 2016.

viewed, nobody should ever, ever expect these kinds of scenes in American politics."[91]

The *New York Times* reported on the violence at the rally, and noted "Video from Los Angeles-area television stations and photographs from the *Los Angeles Times* captured the mayhem, including efforts by some of the mostly young protesters to turn over a patrol car."   It also reminded readers, "Concerns about violence have shadowed Trump rallies across the country, most notably in Chicago in March, when the candidate canceled an appearance as supporters and opponents clashed inside the auditorium."[92]

The Orange County District Attorney charged a 19-year-old resident of Anaheim with "one felony count of vandalism with damage over $400, and one misdemeanor count of inciting a riot," due to his actions after the rally in Costa Mesa. If convicted, the defendant faced "a maximum sentence of three years in Orange County jail."[93] The defendant would later plead guilty to "one misdemeanor count of vandalism with damage over $400 and one misdemeanor count

---

91 MSNBC: The Rachel Maddow Show. Aired April 29th, 2016.
92 Kenny, Steve. "Protest Turns Violent at Donald Trump Rally in Costa Mesa, Calif." *New York Times*. April 30th, 2016.
93 Orange County (California) District Attorney. Press Release: "Man Charged and Arraigned for Throwing Object That Damaged CHP Patrol Vehicle and Inciting Riot at Donald Trump Rally." May 2nd, 2016.

of inciting a riot." He was sentenced to "one year in county jail suspended, 12 days in county jail, three years of informal probation, and was ordered to pay restitution."[94] The reaction to Donald Trump's rally in Costa Mesa was officially declared a riot.

Fred Whitaker, the Chairman of the Orange County Republican Party, appeared on Fox Business to discuss the violence at rallies in California. "The Left in California is like the Left anywhere else," stated the chairman. "They are using Alinskyite tactics to silence people they do not agree with." When asked about the composition of the protesters, the chairman said, "If you take a look at the 19 people that were arrested in Costa Mesa, they were all millennials, in the 19 to 23 year-old range. They all want supposedly bigger government, and the bigger government they got was riot police. I think they probably all had Common Core literature classes and do not understand irony."

After the winner-takes-all primary in Indiana, Donald Trump earned all 57 delegates from the state to become the presumptive nominee on May 3rd, 2016. Republican National Committee Chairman

---

[94] Orange County (California) District Attorney. Press Release: "Man Convicted of Throwing Object that Damaged CHP Patrol Vehicle and Inciting Riot at Donald Trump Rally." February 17, 2017.

Reince Priebus declared on Twitter Donald Trump was the presumptive nominee, and urged Republicans to focus on defeating Hillary Clinton. Senator Cruz suspended his campaign.[95] The *San Diego Union-Tribune* had called on the leadership and members of the Republican Party to "do a lot of self-examination." The newspaper essentially endorsed Hillary Clinton at that point. When Republicans were deciding whether to back Donald Trump in the general election, the Editorial Board told them to "heed prominent conservatives like George Will and conclude that Trump is unimaginable and unacceptable as commander-in-chief."[96] Despite the *San Diego Union-Tribune*'s plea, later that week, Congressman Issa released a statement saying: "Donald Trump is the obvious choice for every American suffering from eight years of disastrous economic policies and anti-job regulations that have caused real pain to tens of millions of Americans who need and deserve better." When reporting on the endorsement, the *San Diego Union-Tribune* felt it had to clarify "Issa's news release didn't specifically say he was endorsing Trump, but a staffer said the

---

[95] Glueck, Katie. "Ted Cruz Drops Out of Presidential Race." Politico. May 3rd, 2016.
[96] The Editorial Board. "But Seriously, What Does the GOP do About Donald Trump?" *San Diego Union-Tribune*. May 4th, 2016.

congressman intended the announcement as an endorsement."[97]

The *San Diego Union-Tribune* Editorial Board warned readers that the "Trumpocalypse" could happen. The newspaper hoped that Hillary Clinton could understand and turn the tide on the appetite for outsider candidates driven by "economic anxiety, nativism, anger over rapid cultural changes, the sense that Washington is broken or a toxic mix of disillusionment." Donald Trump could win, and assuming otherwise only made his chances better, warned the Editorial Board.[98] The *Orange County Register* Editorial Board was much more optimistic, noting "the looming Trump-Clinton duel presents a massive clash of policies and styles that will encourage citizen participation." It asked its readers: "Isn't that what democracy is about?"[99]

Donald Trump released his list of delegates from California on May 9th, 2016. In the California primary, delegates are awarded based on the results in the state's 53 congressional districts and a state-wide count. The highest-ranking Republican official

---

[97] Stewart, Joshua. "Darrell Issa Says Donald Trump is 'Obvious Choice.'" *San Diego Union-Tribune.* May 5th, 2016.

[98] The Editorial Board. "Beware of the Trumpocalypse: It Could Happen." *San Diego Union-Tribune.* May 5th, 2016.

[99] The Editorial Board. "California Denied the Nomination Spotlight Again." *Orange County Register.* May 5th, 2016.

on the list was Congressman Kevin McCarthy, the Majority Leader, and therefore the second-ranking Republican in the U.S. House of Representatives. Both of San Diego's Republican congressmen, Darrell Issa and Duncan Hunter, were on the list. Other prominent Republicans on the list included State Senate Republican leader Jean Fuller, California Republican Party vice chair Harmeet Dhillon, former Congressman Doug Ose, and former State Senator Tony Strickland.[100] Two days later, Congressman Issa appeared on CNN to discuss hesitation from other Republicans to support Donald Trump. He praised Donald Trump for "helping raise money to retain a Republican Senate and House so he can get things done." At this point, Congressman Issa did not know that he would be in one of the contests needing so much money. In response to Mitt Romney's speech denouncing Donald Trump, he also said, "Mitt [Romney] right now needs to get over the fact that, in fact, somebody he did not pick won."[101]

As California Republicans began to unite behind Trump, Orange County continued to tilt to the left. Santa Ana College was the first college in Orange

---

[100] Blood, Michael. "Some Big-Name California Republicans among Trump Delegates." Associated Press. May 10th, 2016.
[101] CNN: The Situation Room with Wolf Blitzer. Aired 06:00-07:00PM EST on May 11th, 2016.

County to waive tuition for students who graduated from the local school district.   An editorial in the *Orange County Register* on May 11th praised the move because "financial aid for higher education is best handled at the state level." Senator Sanders promised voters free college tuition at all public colleges and universities, which the campaign expected to cost $75 billion per year. Hillary Clinton planned to increase college financial aid by $35 billion per year. The editorial criticized these plans for subsidizing administrative bloat, not reducing it. Although the editorial noted "The high cost of college has become an issue in the presidential contest," it did not mention the impact of college debt on congressional districts.   The University of California, San Diego campus is partially in the 49th Congressional District, and now both Orange County and San Diego County had tuition-waiver programs for graduates of local high schools.[102]   A congressional candidate more closely aligned with Senator Sanders could likely get more turnout among students than a Democrat candidate aligned to Hillary Clinton or a generic Republican candidate.

---

[102] The Editorial Board. "Sensible Approach to Free College."
Orange County Register. May 11th, 2016.

On May 13th, the *San Diego Union-Tribune* published an editorial sharply criticizing Donald Trump's criticisms of Jeff Bezos for using the *Washington Post* "for political purposes to save Amazon in terms of taxes and in terms of anti-trust." The newspaper called this "fascist rhetoric" and "a belligerent form of authoritarianism that should have no place in a healthy democracy." Donald Trump was labeled "a toxic avenger" that is "full of grievances and eager to act upon them, mocking and bullying anyone who gets in his way, bellowing threats at other nations, and expressing contempt for both democratic norms and norms of personal behavior." The editorial ended with the statement: "We hope enough Americans figure this out before Nixon-on-steroids occupies 1600 Pennsylvania Ave."[103]

Senator Sanders returned to San Diego County for a rally in National City on Saturday, May 21st. The *New York Times* mentioned the rally in an article about Senator Sanders' feud with the Democratic Party leadership. More focus was placed on the candidate's visit to International Friendship Park along the U.S.-Mexico border. There, Senator Sanders

---

[103] The Editorial Board. "Donald Trump's Alarming Comments on Jeff Bezos, Amazon." *San Diego Union-Tribune.* May 13th, 2016.

"walked along two large walls separating the countries with an immigration activist and Maria Puga, a woman whose husband was killed by border patrol agents as he attempted a crossing from Mexico."[104] On Twitter, the Sanders campaign called Friendship Park "a meeting place for separated families between the U.S. and Mexico." The Sanders campaign used its proximity to the U.S. southern border to issue statements about immigration. In terms of enforcing existing laws, the Sanders campaign tweeted: "Together, we're going to end our current deportation policies. Our approach to immigration should be to unite families, not divide families." In terms of allowing more people into the country, the Sanders campaign subsequently tweeted: "When children come from war-torn countries in Central America, our job is to give them freedom and security here in the United States." However, as soon as the children were in the United States, Senator Sanders advocated allowing the rest of the family in. The Sanders campaign later tweeted: "What I saw at the US-Mexico border was the fact that you've got children on the one side and their mothers on the other. That's wrong."

---

[104] Alcindor, Yamiche. "Bernie Sanders' Feud with the Democratic Leadership Heats Up." *New York Times*. May 22nd, 2016.

On Sunday, Senator Sanders held rallies in Vista, which is in the 49th Congressional District, and Irvine. The Irvine Meadows Amphitheater is less than 15 miles from the northern boundary of the 49th Congressional District. The *Orange County Register* reported that the 16,000-seat venue was "nearly full."[105] The *Washington Post* reported that the candidate "talked about the fight to end 'starvation wages' and the economic plight of Native Americans." He mostly avoided directly attacking Secretary Clinton. Senator Sanders was quoted as saying "We will be holding rallies up and down the state, the central part of the state, that we think will bring out at least 200,000 people." The candidate had asked rally attendees to secure "a large number" of California's 475 delegates, but the *Washington Post* claimed "No poll has shown Sanders in the position to do that."[106]

The California Secretary of State published voter registration per congressional district as of May

---

[105] Haire, Chris; Roosevelt, Margot; and Wisckol, Martin. "Bernie Sanders in Orange County: Thousands Turn Out to Hear Him Campaign Against 'Rigged' System." *Orange County Register*. May 23rd, 2016.

[106] Weigel, David. "Sanders Barnstorms California with Little to Say about Clinton." *Washington Post*. May 23rd, 2016.

23rd, 2016.[107]   Over the previous 45 calendar days, total voter registration increased by 15,000 voters in the 49th Congressional District.   Total Democrat registrations increased by 9,000 voters, while total Republican registrations only increased by 5,000 voters.   The Republican registration advantage dropped to 30,000 voters. Since the previous primary election that included a presidential primary contest, Democratic Party registrations had increased 9.35%, whereas Republican Party registrations had decreased by 6.88%. Registrations with other political parties or un-affiliated registrations increased by 1.90%. Although registration numbers were favorable for the Democratic Party, commentators began to wonder about the ability to turn Sanders supporters into loyal Democrats. The *New York Times* reported there were "plenty of signs that Senator Bernie Sanders of Vermont has left a mark on the political moment," but some within the Democratic Party began "to worry that as Mr. Sanders continues his quest for the nomination, his chance to build a lasting legacy may be slipping away." After the failed 1988 campaign of Pat Robertson, the so-called Christian Coalition was formed "using his mailing lists and leftover cash to

---

[107] California Secretary of State. Report of Registration by Congressional District: May 3rd, 2016.

build a grass-roots organization, publish conservative voter guides, and promote candidates at every level." Instead of converting his soon-to-end campaign into a lasting movement, "Mr. Sanders is wrapped up in the race itself, sharpening his attacks on Hillary Clinton and demanding she debate him before the June 7 primary in California." The newspaper speculated the "disparate individuals and volunteer groups" bought to the Democratic Party by the Sanders campaign "might be inclined to go their separate ways after the primary."[108] During the Vista rally, Senator Sanders was quoted saying, "Our vision of social justice, of economic justice, of racial justice and of environmental justice—our vision is the future of this country, and I hope the leadership of the Democratic Party understands it must be the vision of the Democratic Party."[109] The *Washington Post* determined the "squeamishness" of Sanders supporters to remain with the Democratic Party after Hillary Clinton wins the nomination "may be her top challenge as she turns toward her general-election

---

[108] Mahler, Jonathan; Alcindor, Yamiche. "Fixated on Campaign Fight, Sanders Risks Lasting Legacy." *New York Times*. May 23rd, 2016.

[109] Chozick, Amy. "Clinton Stresses Need to Challenge Trump." *New York Times*. May 23rd, 2016.

battle against Donald Trump."[110] Assuming Sanders supporters abandoned Hillary Clinton in the general election, the next uncertainty would be whether or not they even go to the polls for down-ballot candidates. Losing Sanders supporters might not be an issue for Hillary Clinton in California, but it would certainly have an impact on other candidates, such as Colonel Applegate. The Sanders campaign had a different view. A press release stated: "The surge in Democratic voter registration will benefit down ballot races, with many districts seeing 10 percent or more of their voting population registering to vote in the last 90 days." Alluding to Senator Sanders' future role in the party, the press release added: "With high turn out and a large swath or new progressive voters, Sanders has excited the future of the Party to help Democrats win across the board in California."[111] Nationally, Republicans continued to lose ground on the generic ballot. A NBC News/Wall Street Journal Survey in May of 1,000 registered voters found that 48% of respondents preferred a Democrat-controlled Congress in the upcoming election, whereas only 44% of respondents preferred a Republican-controlled

---

[110] Weigel, David. "Why so Many Sanders Supporters Don't Want to Be Democrats." *Washington Post.* May 25th, 2016.

[111] Bernie Sanders Campaign Press Release: "California Voter Registration Surges Under Sanders Candidacy." May 18th, 2016.

Congress. The remaining 8% were undecided.[112] Compared to the survey from April, Democrats gained one point and Republicans lost one point. If the 49th Congressional District mirrored the national mood, then Congressman Issa's partisan affiliation was becoming more of a liability than an asset in the upcoming election.

An editorial in the *Orange County Register* on May 24th noted Senator Sanders "is garnering support not only in California's more liberal areas, but also in the more conservative and Republican precincts in Orange, San Bernardino and Riverside counties." The people supporting Senator Sanders also "remain largely passionate and upbeat, even though his path to the nomination at July's Democratic Convention in Philadelphia is nearly impossible." The editorial speculated Senator Sanders' only path to the nomination was to win big in California and convince Clinton-aligned superdelegates to change their endorsements. Senator Sanders' determination to stay in the race through the California primary "spells trouble for Democrats trying to rally the party around Mrs. Clinton, who in recent polls was running even with

---

[112] NBC News/Wall Street Journal Survey. Study #16306. Date Range: May 15th-19th, 2016.

Mr. Trump." In contrast, the editorial noted Donald Trump had mostly quieted the "Never Trump" movement within the Republican Party. The Anaheim Convention Center hosted Senator Sanders on May 24th and Donald Trump on May 25th.[113] The Anaheim Convention Center is less than 30 miles from the northern boundary of the 49th Congressional District. Senator Sanders asked the crowd: "Anybody here working for Disney?" Some in the audience answered in the affirmative. Then, Senator Sanders asked: "Anybody here making a living wage working for Disney?" Many answered negatively. Senator Sanders criticized Disney for paying "its workers wages that are so low that many of them are forced to live in motels because they can't afford a decent place to live," while paying its chairman and chief executive officer Bob Iger over $46 million in one year. The candidate called this an example of a rigged economy.

During the 2016 election cycle, Mr. Iger contributed $25,000 to the Democratic Congressional Campaign Committee in March (before Senator Sanders' Anaheim rally),[114] $25,000 to the Democratic

---

[113] The Editorial Board. "Sanders Fans Make Noise in O.C." *Orange County Register*. May 24th, 2016.
[114] Schedule A (FEC Form 3X) Itemized Receipts. DCCC. Page 5,926 of 15,115.

Senatorial Campaign Committee in July,[115] and $100,000 to the Hillary Victory Fund in August.[116] With the amount of money the Democratic Party was raising from people directly attacked by Senator Sanders, it is no wonder the Democratic Party leadership did not embrace Senator Sanders, and also no wonder Sanders supporters did not trust the Democratic Party leadership.

On the same day as the rally in Anaheim, the Sanders campaign released a new advertisement directed towards Californians. It asked "What choice do Californians have in this election?" Senator Sanders, narrating the ad, replied to that question: "The biggest one of all. You have the power to choose a new direction for the Democratic Party. To break the back of a corrupt system of campaign finance that keeps a rigged economy in place. To stand up to Wall Street and make the wealthy pay their fair share. To fight for tuition-free public colleges and universities."[117]

The *Washington Post* summarized Donald Trump's rally in Anaheim as "a string of attacks that

---

[115] Schedule A (FEC Form 3X) Itemized Receipts. DSCC. Page 671 of 12,860.

[116] Schedule A (FEC Form 3X) Itemized Receipts. Hillary Victory Fund. Page 44,896 of 73,014.

[117] Bernie Sanders Campaign Press Release: "Sanders Releases New California Ad." May 24th, 2016.

played like a greatest-hits collection from the raucous GOP primary contest." The paper reported the candidate "knocked South Carolina Gov. Nikki Haley's decision to endorse Sen. Marco Rubio, R-Florida, mocked former Florida governor Jeb Bush for his energy level and blasted 2012 Republican presidential nominee Mitt Romney as a 'choker.'"[118] Although he continued to criticize other leaders of the Republican Party, he was doing exceptionally well with the Republican voter base. Donald Trump announced during the Anaheim rally that he had received more votes than any other Republican presidential candidate in history.

On May 26th, 2016, the Associated Press reported that Donald Trump had reached 1,237 delegates, meaning he had enough to formally win the nomination.[119] The next day, Donald Trump held a rally in San Diego. While preparing for the rally, Congressman Issa appeared on Fox News. Guest host Charles Payne asked him about Donald Trump's decision that day to not debate Senator Sanders, who at that time was still competing against Hillary Clinton for the Democratic Party nomination.

---

[118] DelReal, Jose; Johnson, Jenna. "Trump Continues to Bash GOP Rivals." *Washington Post.* May 25th, 2016.

[119] Ohlemacher, Stephen. "Mister 1,237: North Dakota Delegate Puts Trump Over the Top." Associated Press. May 26th, 2016.

Congressman Issa still supported the idea of a debate, for two reasons. First, Donald Trump required $10 million be raised for charity before participating in the event. Second, Congressman Issa saw the debate as "an opportunity to contrast Bernie Sanders' openly leftist views with [Donald Trump's], particularly since Hillary Clinton has continued to essentially embrace Bernie Sanders and his socialist agenda." He then claimed America "can either go to the left, like Venezuela, and have failure, or we can reinvigorate our economy and have the kind of success we had during the Reagan years." Congressman Issa linked support for Senator Sanders to the impact of college debt on the younger generation of voters.[120] If the burden of college debt was pushing younger voters to the left, that will further push Congressman Issa's district to the left. It includes parts of the University of California, San Diego campus.

During the rally, Congressman Issa made a short speech, only a few minutes in length. His statement, in full, is below:

> *"Are you ready for the next president of the*
> *United States? I see a lot of young faces*
> *here. But over there in the back, I see some*

---

[120] Fox News: Your World with Neil Cavuto. Aired May 27th, 2016.

wrinkled old veterans. I see some people who remember that we have been here before. When I was a private, a young EOD tech in the early seventies, 1970 to be exact, some of those people remember that we were in the longest war in history. We had lost track of what victory was and we were not headed towards victory. But that changed. By the time I was through ROTC and was commissioned, Jimmy Carter was president. For some of those slightly younger crusty old veterans, we have been here before. We had a president who figured we could run the military for less and did not understand the most expensive military is the one that is not ready; and the least expensive military is the one that keeps you free, and out of war. Those veterans know that. So we have been there before, and I want to tell you: We are here again. We are here at the same moment as when I was a captain leaving active duty, in 1980. Jimmy Carter was still president. A man was running who was not part of inside-Washington politics. And he was vilified. They even called him 'Ronald Raygun.' Those old crusty guys remember this. We have been here before in which they wanted to demonize someone because they said it like it is, they meant what they said, and they came to Washington to do what they said they were going to do. Now, many of you have signs that say 'Trump-Reagan.' The fact is, you need to think that way, because we are here again, and the only way we are going to get our economy going again, the way Ronald Reagan did, is with somebody like Donald Trump. And the only way we are going to make America great and safe again, and end these wars through victory, is with Donald Trump. So on this weekend in which we gather both to honor the next president of the United States and to celebrate the men and women that I had the honor to come after, and I had the honor to come before, in the military, for you, we will elect Donald Trump the next president of the United States, and make America great again!"

During the rally, Donald Trump claimed he had gotten a call from Congressman Issa a few weeks prior, "long before people thought we would be winning this so quickly." In the call, according to Donald Trump, Congressman Issa said, "Donald, I endorse you 100%." Donald Trump thanked Congressman Issa, then thanked Congressman Hunter. Then, he gave his endorsement of both candidates, saying: "You better vote for these guys forever, we're never letting them go."

Before the primary, Congressman Issa continued to focus on the national presidential race, not his own congressional race. In the week prior to the primary, he criticized Hillary Clinton in an interview with the *San Diego Union-Tribune*. He said: "Testimony before our (House Oversight and Government Reform) committee makes it clear that she may have stayed awake all night, but she was frozen in place (during the Benghazi attacks in 2012). It's important because Hillary Clinton was there to make the mistakes before 9/11, during 9/11 -- and be part of the cover-ups and lies about 9/11."[121]

Only three candidates declared their candidacy to contest the 49th Congressional District, with one of them not being aligned with any political party and having not spent any money. It was very unlikely that Congressman Issa would not be one of the top-two candidates to advance to the general election.

---

[121] Steele, Jeanette. "What People Are Saying About Clinton in San Diego." *San Diego Union-Tribune*. June 3rd, 2016.

Regardless, he did not seem to be focused on driving up turnout before the primary.

Both candidates were required to disclose campaign finance data up to May 18th in their Pre-Primary Report to the Federal Election Commission. By that point in the campaign, Congressman Issa had out-raised Colonel Applegate more than 13-to-1 and out-spent him almost 15-to-1. Issa for Congress so far had raised $731,000, spent $655,000, and had $3.7 million cash on hand.[122] During the period, almost half of the campaign's expenditures went to strategic and fundraising consulting services.[123] Applegate for Congress had raised $54,000, spent $43,000, and had $10,000 cash on hand.[124]

On the ballot, there was only one contest for a state-wide office: The U.S. Senate seat to replace Democrat Barbara Boxer. There was only one proposition on the ballot: Proposition 50. It dealt with suspending legislators.

California uses the top-two open primary system for all elected offices, except for the state-wide presidential primary. The California Democratic

---

[122] Filing FEC-1074704. Form 3: Pre-Primary. Filed May 26th, 2016.

[123] Filing FEC-1074704. Schedule B. Filed May 26th, 2016.

[124] Filing FEC-1151322. Form 3: Pre-Primary. Amendment 2. Filed March 3rd, 2017.

Party allowed voters with no party preference to request a cross-over ballot to participate in the Democratic Party primary. The California Republican Party decided to only allow registered Republicans to vote in the Republican Party primary. Of the 395,000 voters with no party preference throughout San Diego County, 75,000 of them requested cross-over ballots to participate in the Democratic Party primary. Throughout Orange County, 56,000 of the total 314,000 voters with no party preference did so. [125]

San Diego County and Orange County have five Republican representatives in Congress: Ed Royce (39th), Mimi Walters (45th), Dana Rohrabacher (48th), Darrell Issa (49th), and Duncan Hunter (50th). Congressman Royce only had one Democrat opponent. Congressman Rohrabacher faced two Democrat opponents. Congresswoman Walters faced two Democrat opponents and one Republican opponent. Congressman Hunter faced two Democrat opponents, one Republican opponent, and one non-aligned opponent. Only Congressman Issa faced one Democrat opponent and one non-aligned opponent. According to the chairwoman of the San Diego County Democratic Party, no one formally associated

---

[125] California Secretary of State: "No Party Preference (NPP) Voter Cross-Over Ballot Requests – June 7, 2016, Presidential Primary Election."

with the party was interested in running against Congressman Issa, because of the perception that he could not be beaten. [126]

In the last editorial before the California primary, the *San Diego Union-Tribune* Editorial Board was conflicted on advising Republican voters. It stated that it could not endorse Donald Trump because of "belligerence, casual cruelty, [and] incoherence on policy issues." It considered not voting at all to be a waste, but also stated voting for another candidate accomplished nothing. Instead, the paper encouraged Republicans to write in Ronald Reagan for president. In contrast with President Reagan, candidate Donald Trump was "the Great Excommunicator." [127] This request does not appear to have actually had an impact on the primary.

---

[126] Spagat, Elliot; Blood, Michael. "California GOP Congressman Darrell Issa Narrowly Wins Seat." *Canadian Press*. November 28, 2016.

[127] The Editorial Board. "California GOP Voters, Send Donald Trump this Message." *San Diego Union-Tribune*. June 3rd, 2016.

CHAPTER 4: JUNE 7TH, 2016 – THE CALIFORNIA PRIMARY

Congressman Royce was the most popular Republican candidate, winning 60.5% of the vote in his district.   Congressman Rohrabacher was the second most popular Republican candidate, winning 56.6% of the vote. Republican candidates captured the highest percent of the vote in the 50th Congressional District, winning 63.3% of the vote, although 56.5% came from Congressman Hunter. Congresswoman Walters was the least popular Republican candidate, winning only 40.9% of the vote. However, the combined Republican share of the vote was 60.1% in the 45th Congressional District.

On Tuesday's primary, Congressman Issa only won 50.8% of the vote, meaning the 49th Congressional District was also the most vulnerable

Republican-held district in the region. Colonel Applegate came in second, with 45.5% of the vote.[128]

Despite Congressman Issa receiving less than 50% of the vote in the portion of the district that belongs to San Diego County, Republicans celebrated when the Democrat incumbent for the Board of Supervisors District 3 received only 38.7% of the vote. Republican Encinitas Mayor Kristin Gaspar came in second with 34.2% of the vote.[129] Encinitas lies within the 49th Congressional District.

Twelve Republicans contested the U.S. Senate seat, but none of them received more than 7.8% of the vote. California Attorney General Kamala Harris, a Democrat, came in first with 39.9% of the vote. Congresswoman Loretta Sanchez, also a Democrat, came in second, with 18.9% of the vote. Both of them, despite being in the same political party, advanced to the general election. Proposition 50 passed state-wide with 75.6% of voters approving. In San Diego County and Orange County, it passed with 76.6% and 71.6% of voters approving, respectively.

In the Democrat primary, Hillary Clinton won the 49th Congressional District with 47,105 votes to

---

[128] California Secretary of State. 2016 Primary Election Statement of Vote: United States Representatives.
[129] San Diego County. June 7th, 2016 Presidential Primary Election Official Results.

42,341 votes for Senator Sanders. Combined, Democrat candidates received 89,941 votes within the district. In the Republican primary, Donald Trump won the district with 55,339 votes. Combined, Republican candidates received 70,271 votes within the district. Despite a 30,000 voter registration advantage before the June 7th primary, Democrat presidential candidates received over 19,000 more votes than Republican presidential candidates. This would support the assumption that voters who supported Democratic Party candidates had more of an incentive to show up and vote during the primary than supporters of the Republican Party, because Donald Trump was already the presumptive nominee.

As of that Friday, Colonel Applegate was still answering his own campaign phone line when called by the media,[130] but he soon hired a team of full-time campaigners.[131] The Democratic Congressional Campaign Committee (DCCC) commissioned a poll in the 49th Congressional District. It was conducted on June 15th and 16th. It surveyed 504 likely general

---

[130] Jenkins, Logan. "Logan Jenkins Column." *San Diego Union-Tribune.* June 11th, 2016.
[131] Stewart, Joshua. "Darrell Issa Takes Decisive Lead Over Doug Applegate to Win a Ninth Term." *San Diego Union-Tribune.* November 29th, 2016.

election voters. The pollster did not provide information about the candidates during the survey; likely voters were only asked which of the two candidates they planned to support. Supposedly, the poll found that both candidates polled at 43%, with 14% undecided and a 4.36% margin of error. The *San Diego Union-Tribune* reported on the poll on June 21st. Jonathan Wilcox, a spokesman for Congressman Issa, called it "an absurd push poll from the Democratic Party, with trumped-up numbers and results manipulated in their favor." He stated that Congressman Issa won the primary election by almost 10,000 votes, and expected to win again in November.[132] The campaign also tweeted on June 21st: "There they go again: Dems also pushed bogus CA-49 poll in 2014; we won that election by 20 points."

Throughout the general election, commentators discussed the relationship between the presidential candidate and the congressional candidate on the ballot. It is quite common for voters to enter the voting booth to vote for a presidential candidate, but not completely fill out the ballot. In the 49th Congressional District, 89,941 votes were cast

---

[132] Stewart, Joshua. "Democratic Polls Shows Applegate, Issa Tied." *San Diego Union-Tribune.* June 21st, 2016.

for Democratic Party presidential candidates, but Colonel Applegate only received 75,808 votes. Assuming that everyone who voted for Colonel Applegate also voted for a Democratic Party presidential nominee, then only 84% of people that voted for a Democratic Party presidential nominee bothered to continue down the ballot for the congressional race. On the Republican Party ballot in the 49th Congressional District, 55,339 votes were cast for Donald Trump, 70,271 votes were cast for all Republican Party presidential nominees, and 84,626 votes were cast for Congressman Issa. Assuming that everyone who voted for a Republican Party presidential candidate also voted for Congressman Issa, then only 83% of people that voted further down the ballot bothered to fill in the top of the ticket. The relationship between the top of the ticket and down-ballot races was reversed for Colonel Applegate and Congressman Issa.

After the June 7th primary, Senator Sanders' hopes of obtaining the Democratic Party's presidential nomination was over. However, at a rally in Santa Monica, he declared he would "take the fight for social, economic and racial justice to

Philadelphia" as the campaign fights "for every vote and every delegate."[133]

Later that month, the San Diego Regional Chamber hosted its Annual Congressional Luncheon. Democrat Congresswoman Davis, Democrat Congressman Peters, Republican Congressman Issa, and Republican Congressman Hunter attended. The *San Diego Union-Tribune* quoted Congressman Issa saying: "Donald Trump got this job because [President Obama] has been so polarizing." Congressman Hunter, who was the second member of the House of Representatives to endorse Donald Trump, stated he will not be attending the Republican Party's convention in Cleveland. He speculated it would be "mayhem and riots and hooligans and thugs and police forces. And that is just the actual convention." Congressman Peters was quoted as saying that betting money was on Hillary Clinton winning, and the newspaper noted "Neither Hunter nor Issa made any sort of statement at the luncheon indicating that they believe Trump will win November's election."[134]

---

[133] Bernie Sanders Campaign Press Release: "The Struggle Continues." June 8th, 2016.
[134] Stewart, Joshua. "Some Prominent California Trump Backers Have Buyer's Remorse." *San Diego Union-Tribune.* June 21st, 2016.

Congressman Issa finished June still focused more on national issues than campaigning. He joined eight other Republican Congressmen from California in signing a letter addressed to the Obama administration in response to California's waiver application to give illegal immigrants the ability to buy health insurance through Covered California, the state's exchange. The *Orange County Register* reported on the letter on June 30th.[135]

By the end of the second quarter of 2016, Issa for Congress had raised $845,000, spent $759,000, and had $3.7 million cash on hand.[136] The Issa campaign incurred costs related to the upcoming Republican National Convention in Cleveland, Ohio.[137] His continued relationship with Donald Trump would later be used against him. Applegate for Congress had raised $188,000, spent $50,000, and had $138,000 cash on hand.[138] About one-quarter of donations to Applegate for Congress during the period came from

---

[135] Kopetman, Roxana. "Orange County's GOP Congress Members Fight Health Care Expansion to Immigrants." *Orange County Register*. June 30th, 2016.

[136] Filing FEC-1084849. Form 3: July Quarterly. Filed July 14th, 2016.

[137] Filing FEC-1084849. Schedule B. Filed July 14th, 2016.

[138] Filing FEC-1151324. Form 3: July Quarterly. Filed March 3rd, 2017.

San Diego (especially La Jolla), which is not in the district.[139]

One month after the June 7th primary, the California Secretary of State published voter registrations by congressional district. The Republican voter registration advantage had fallen below 30,000 voters in the 49th Congressional District. Overall registrations increased, but Democratic Party registrations increased almost twice as fast as Republican Party registrations. Interestingly, Federal Election Commission financial disclosures indicate Issa for Congress paid over $15,000 on July 1st to the Tarrance Group to perform polling. The results of the poll were never released by the Issa campaign, indicating the resulting poll showed that Colonel Applegate was winning.

The Republican National Convention was held in Cleveland, in July. Congressman Issa attended as part of the California delegation. The year 2016 was unique for the California delegation to the Republican National Convention. Swing states and reliably Republican states are usually allocated seats towards the front of the arena, with reliably Democrat states like California near the back. Many large or influential states have delegates pledged to multiple

---

[139] Filing FEC-1151324. Schedule A. Filed March 3rd, 2017.

candidates. Because of the way the rules were written for California's delegates, the Trump campaign picked 169 of the 172 delegates. The three delegates not chosen by the Trump campaign were also pro-Trump. That made the California delegation both the largest and likely the most unified in support of Donald Trump. The California delegation was put directly in front of the stage, so that television cameras could capture the delegation's unified enthusiasm.[140]

On the first day, Congressman Issa appeared on Fox News to discuss the convention. Although the host wanted to focus on the "Lock her up!" chants heard from the crowd, Congressman Issa pivoted the conversation to positives about Donald Trump. He said: "We Republicans have to make a case for how we will make America great again, not just help with the economy, by getting out of the way, but also around the world, a foreign policy, a national defense structure that has America assert its historic position of leadership to help free 22-plus nations that are now

---

[140] Wisckol, Martin. "Republican National Convention: California Delegates—So Far, Yet So Near." *Orange County Register*. July 19th, 2016.

struggling with ISIS, and many other problems around the world."[141]

The next day, the *Orange County Register* reported on Congressman Issa's comments about Senator Cruz's refusal to directly endorse Donald Trump at the convention. "Last night, we made it clear to those who are not on the train that we are not stopping until we get to the station in November," he was quoted as saying during remarks to the California delegation.[142]

Senator Rubio, who was Congressman Issa's preferred candidate, endorsed Donald Trump at the convention. "After a long and spirited primary, the time for fighting each other is over," said Senator Rubio in a pre-recorded video. He concluded the endorsement by saying: "It is time to come together and fight for a new direction for America. It is time to win in November."

After helping Donald Trump collect endorsements at the Republican National Convention, Congressman Issa was back in San Diego to pick up a local endorsement. On July 28th, the San Diego Regional Chamber of Commerce held a regular

---

[141] Fox News: Your World with Neil Cavuto. Aired July 20th, 2016.

[142] Wisckol, Martin. "GOP Convention: Darrell Issa's Distain for Ted Cruz." *Orange County Register*. July 21st, 2016.

meeting. The Board of Directors asked questions to Congressman Issa after his prepared remarks. Later, the Board of Directors voted to endorse a slate of candidates from both parties, including Congressman Issa.[143]

Nationally, Republicans came out of the their convention much more united than expected. Donald Trump was the Republican nominee. Now, Congressman Issa had to adapt to whatever positive or negative influences that would have on his re-election.

---

[143] Phillips, Alison. "Chamber Makes Three New Endorsements in November Races." San Diego Regional Chamber of Commerce. August 1st, 2016.

CHAPTER 5: AUGUST – THREE MONTHS UNTIL THE GENERAL ELECTION

Startup Day Across America was held on August 4th, 2016, the program's fourth year. Congressman Issa visited The Control Group, which provides a consumer-facing background check website. The company had been negatively impacted by abuse of the H1B work visa program, which Congressman Issa introduced legislation to reform. He later visited Airbitz, which provides software that encrypts consumer data. The company benefited from the newly enacted Title III of the JOBS Act, which allows companies to sell equity stakes to more than just accredited investors. Last, he visited the Belching Beaver Brewery. Congressman Issa at that point had co-sponsored a bill that would reduce the excise tax on beer.[144]

The next evening, Congressman Issa appeared on Fox News to discuss Federal Bureau of Investigations Director James Comey's responses to questions about Hillary Clinton's emails. Director Comey stated Hillary Clinton made false claims about having and sending classified material via her private email. Congressman Issa summed up this election cycle as "a question of trust versus the other idiosyncrasies." Later in the interview, on the topic of Donald Trump endorsing Speaker Paul Ryan, Congressman Issa presented himself as a representative of California Republicans. He stated, "it is my hope that Donald Trump will see that in fact in this very diverse party, you have to endorse, if you will, all wings of the party, because the people in Louisiana, the people in Wisconsin, and those of us in California, we are Republicans, yes, but we are also a very diverse party."[145]

While Congressman Issa was discussing Hillary Clinton's troubles with the Federal Bureau of Investigations on national media, local media ran a

---

[144] Van Grove, Jennifer. "Tech and Beer: Congressman Samples Local Startup Life." *San Diego Union-Tribune*. August 5th, 2016.
[145] Fox News: Your World with Neil Cavuto. Aired August 5th, 2016.

story on the "growing signs that veteran Rep. Darrell Issa, R-Vista, could be headed for an election dogfight." The article noted the fact that the Republican voter registration advantage was shrinking. It also speculated that Congressman Issa's support for Donald Trump could undermine his chances, whereas "his Democratic opponent's background as a Marine colonel holds particular appeal in a district that includes and surrounds Camp Pendleton." Readers of the *Orange County Register* were reminded that Congressman Issa "introduced Trump at a San Diego rally, was a Trump delegate to the Republican National Convention and [...] spoke supportively of Trump during his visits with California, Illinois and North Carolina convention delegations." So far in the race, the events of note for Colonel Applegate were the DCCC's June poll that showed the candidates tied and the fact that the DCCC had indicated it might add California's 49th Congressional District to its list of targeted seats held by Republicans. Congressman Issa's strengths were his cash balance, which was reported at $3.8 million.

Although the article noted "Democratic turnout was proportionately bigger than usual in the state's primary, to a large extent because Democrats had a competitive primary while the GOP contest was settled," it did not mention the fact that Colonel

Applegate received fewer votes than top-of-the-ticket Democrat candidates, whereas Congressman Issa received more votes than top-of-the-ticket Republican candidates.[146]

On August 15th, the Issa campaign tweeted a picture of campaign yard signs, telling volunteers that yard signs were available upon request. That same day, the Mayor of Carlsbad endorsed Congressman Issa for re-election, stating he "has been an invaluable asset to us here in Carlsbad." In response to the endorsement, Congressman Issa said, "One of the greatest joys I have in Congress is getting to collaborate with local officials to find fresh solutions to the problems our local communities are facing."[147]

Carlsbad was critical to Congressman Issa's campaign. The city had 25,000 registered Republicans, and contributed about 20% of the district's overall Republican voter registration after the June primary.

The day after the Mayor of Carlsbad's endorsement, the *San Diego Union-Tribune* reported that Congressman Issa worked the register at a gas station in Oceanside at the invitation of the National

---

[146] Wisckol, Martin. "Veteran Rep. Issa Could Face Tough Re-Election Bid." *Orange County Register*. August 5th, 2016
[147] Issa For Congress Press Release: "Carlsbad Mayor Matt Hall Endorses Darrell Issa for Congress." August 16th, 2016.

Association of Convenience Stores. The trade association had also invited Democrat Congressman Scott Peters to a gas station in his district as part of the same program. The laws passed related to selling "tobacco, alcohol, hazardous materials, packaged food, prepared food, raw food, and motor fuel" directly impact convenience stores. Convenience stores can have an impact on local politics. When Congressman Issa participated in the event, there were approximately 220 convenience stores in his district.[148] In an election determined by about 1,600 votes, appealing to the voters whose livelihood depended on the 220 convenience stores in the district might have been one of many activities throughout the campaign that got Congressman Issa across the finish line.

According to the Issa campaign's Twitter account, the campaign kickoff event was held at OC Tavern in San Clemente. Activists that attended the event had 77 calendar days to drive higher turnout among Republicans to help Congressman Issa get enough votes in November.

Colonel Applegate's first advertised endorsement was Sandra Fluke, who the press release

---

[148] Stewart, Joshua. "Rep. Issa Works as Gas Station Clerk. Kind of." *San Diego Union-Tribune.* August 17th, 2016.

referred to as a social justice attorney. She had been invited to speak by Democrat congressional committee members during a hearing chaired by Congressman Issa on the Affordable Care Act's mandated coverage of contraceptives. Congressman Issa claimed her name had been submitted too late. At that time, Sandra Fluke was described by the *Washington Post* as "a third-year student at Georgetown Law and past president of the school's Students for Reproductive Justice group."[149] Besides being anti-Issa, it is unclear what connection she had to the 49th Congressional District.

In late August, the *Orange County Register* published an article about Republican elected officials distancing themselves from Donald Trump. Assemblywoman Ling Ling Chang, who was seeking a state senate seat that represents parts of Orange County, said "Trump has made so many outrageous and offensive comments that they are too numerous to mention," and told the paper she was "going to focus on doing my job in the Assembly and my own campaign." A spokesperson for Assemblywoman Young Kim, who was seeking re-election, stated on behalf of the candidate: "She is not involving herself

---

[149] Kliff, Sarah. "The Woman You Didn't Hear at Congress' Contraceptives Hearing." *Washington Post*. February 16th, 2012.

in the presidential campaign, so will have no comment," on the national election. The Republican Main Street Advocacy group held a "Women2Women Conversation" lunch program in Irvine, the third largest city in Orange County, also in late August. Main Street President Sarah Chamberlain, Congresswoman Mimi Walters, and Board of Equalization Member Diane Harkey answered questions about mental health reform, young voter engagement, sexual assault legislation, Republican legislative goals, down-ticket candidates, and women's involvement in politics, but Trump's name never came up. A reporter for the *Orange County Register* asked the host of the event what she told women who expressed reservations with candidate Donald Trump. Sarah Chamberlain replied: "We encourage them to turn out and vote down ticket and do what they think is best at the top of the ticket."[150] That comment was almost directly targeted towards Congressman Issa's district. Donald Trump was likely not going to win the state-wide contest for California's Electoral College votes, but the Republican Party still needed people to show up and

---

[150] Wisckol, Martin. "Two GOP Candidates Steer Clear of Donald Trump." *Orange County Register*. August 20th, 2016.

vote for Congressman Issa and other down-ballot offices.

A few days later, the *San Diego Union-Tribune* ran a story about Donald Trump's influence on elections in San Diego County. The article expanded on a newsletter the San Diego Democratic Party sent out claiming "Republicans in San Diego County are either making excuses for Trump, scrambling for cover, or racing for the exits." The article put Congressman Issa in the "making excuses" category. Denise Gitsham, the Republican challenger to the Democrat incumbent in the 52nd Congressional District, was put in the "scrambling for cover" category after stating Donald Trump had not yet earned her vote. Kristin Gaspar, the incumbent Republican Encinitas Mayor that was running for County Supervisor, was put in the "racing for the exits" category after voting for Donald Trump in the primary, but then stressing that she had never endorsed him and that he had lost her vote in November.[151]

At the end of August, Strategies 360 conducted a survey on behalf of Applegate for Congress among 599 likely voters in the 49th Congressional District.

---

[151] Jenkins, Logan. "The Trump Factor in SD Races." *San Diego Union-Tribune.* August 25th, 2016.

The survey reported Congressman Issa narrowly led with 45% support against Colonel Applegate's 43% support. The margin of error was 4%, and 13% of voters were undecided. Although this poll showed Congressman Issa's support had increased since the last poll was conducted in June, Colonel Applegate was still within the margin of error. Even though two months had passed since the primary, the voter dynamic reflected by this poll had not changed much. Hillary Clinton was shown as leading Donald Trump in the district 46% to 41%, but on a generic ballot, a Republican led a Democrat 46% to 43%.[152] Considering the fact that Donald Trump had performed worse than down-ballot Republicans in the June primary and in the August poll, the same dynamic could be expected to take Congressman Issa across the finish line in a district that Hillary Clinton will win.

The San Diego Registrar of Voters reported there were 98,516 registered Republicans, 90,277 registered Democrats, and 83,767 registered voters not aligned with either major party at the end of August.[153] Between the primary registrations close date on May

---

[152] Strategies 360: "Doug Applegate and Darrell Issa in a Statistical Dead Heat in CA49." August 29th, 2016.
[153] San Diego County Registrar of Voters. "Report of Registration – State Reporting Districts." September 1st, 2016.

23rd and the report at the end of August, Democratic Party registrations increased by 2,207 voters, whereas Republican Party registrations only increased by 678 voters in the San Diego County portion of the district. In a major-party, head-to-head comparison, the Democratic Party in San Diego was winning the registration contest. The number of voters not aligned with either major party increased by 2,748 voters.

CHAPTER 6: SEPTEMBER – TWO MONTHS UNTIL THE GENERAL ELECTION

One issue during the campaign was the regulation of "sober living homes" by local communities. A "sober living home" is a residential care facility for adults who are recovering from alcohol or drug abuse, housing no more than six people. In January of 2008, Newport Beach enacted Ordinance 2008-05 to place limits on the operation of sober living homes. This was in response to the city's findings that it had the highest ratio of licensed recovery beds per resident of any city in Orange County, and likely had the highest amount of residential recovery facilities of any city in California. *Newport Coast Recovery LLC v. City of Newport Beach* was filed in response to the ordinance on June 16th, 2009. Judge James V. Selna, of the United States District Court for the Central District of California, dismissed the lawsuit on March 14th, 2011. Judge Selna was appointed by President George W. Bush in 2003. The case was appealed to the United States Court of Appeals for the Ninth Circuit in 2012. Chief Judge Alex Kozinski, Judge Stephen Reinhardt, and Judge Sidney R. Thomas presided over the appeal. The opinion of the court reversed the lower court's ruling and held "the district court erred in disregarding the evidence that the City's sole objective in enacting and enforcing its Ordinance was to discriminate against persons deemed to be disabled under state and federal housing discrimination laws." Judge Kozinski was nominated by President Reagan in 1985, and at that point was the youngest federal appellate judge appointed in the 20th century.[154] Judge Reinhardt was nominated by Jimmy Carter in 1979, and would later become known as "the liberal face of the U.S. 9th Circuit Court of Appeals."[155] Judge Thomas was nominated by Bill Clinton in 1995. The *Los Angeles Times* reported that he was on President Obama's shortlist of potential Supreme

---

[154] Jackson, Robert L. and Hager, Philip. "Senate Narrowly Confirms Kozinski as Appeals Judge." *Los Angeles Times*. November 8th, 1985.

[155] Dolan, Maura. "Stephen Reinhardt, 'liberal lion' of the 9th Circuit, dies at 87." *Los Angeles Times*. March 29th, 2018.

Court nominees in 2010 to replace Justice Stevens.[156] Newport Beach, a city with almost twice as many registered Republicans as registered Democrats, was told by two of the most left-leaning judges in the country that municipal activities to limit the number of recovering drug addicts in its community was discrimination against people with disabilities. It is easy to see how this law would become an issue in the election.

On the first day of September, Congressman Issa was back in his district, leading a panel in San Clemente to discuss regulation of sober living homes. The *Orange County Register* reported that over 300 people attended. State Senator Pat Bates and Assemblyman Bill Brough, both California legislators that represent parts of the 49th Congressional District, were also on the panel, among others. Congressman Issa used the opportunity to discuss a bill he proposed to amend the Fair Housing Act "to specifically clarify that state or local governments may enact and enforce a zoning ordinances or other regulations that would limit the number of sober

---

[156] Oliphant, James and Parsons, Christi. "Obama Casts a Wide Net; His Search for a Supreme Court Nominee Includes the Nontraditional." *Los Angeles Times*. April 14th, 2010.

homes within a particular neighborhood."[157] The Safe Recovery and Community Empowerment Act was introduced to the House of Representatives as H.R. 6070 on September 20th. The same day, the San Clemente City Council voted 5-0 to direct staff to send a letter in support of Congressman Issa's bill.[158]

On September 8th, 2016, the DCCC announced that it added the 49th Congressional District to its Red to Blue Program, which "highlights top Democratic campaigns across the country, and offers them financial, communications, grassroots, and strategic support." At that point, there were 48 other districts in either the Red to Blue or Emerging Races program.[159] Public Opinion Strategies conducted a poll on behalf of the Issa campaign between September 6th and 8th. This poll found Congressman Issa led with 52% of the vote against Colonel Applegate with 38%. That indicated 10% of voters were undecided. The poll was reported to have a

---

[157] Office of Congressman Darrell Issa Press Release. September 20th, 2016.

[158] City of San Clemente. Special and Regular City Council Meeting – September 20th, 2016.

[159] Democratic Congressional Campaign Committee Press Release: "Marine Colonel Doug Applegate Added to Red to Blue Program." September 8th, 2016.

4.9% margin of error.[160] The next day, the California Secretary of State published updated voter registration statistics that confirmed the 49th Congressional District was increasingly competitive. In the 49th Congressional District, over 360,000 people were registered to vote, an increase of about two thousand registrations since the deadline for the primary. Registrations not affiliated with either major party increased by 2,594 voters, Democratic Party registrations increased by 880 voters, and Republican Party registrations decreased by 1,167 voters. Although the Republican registration advantage still stood at over 28,000 voters, the Democratic Party was winning the registration race.

Between May and September, the Democratic Party had registered more voters than the Republican Party in every city within the district. Only San Clemente, Dana Point, and San Juan Capistrano, the three most Republican-leaning cities in the district, saw net increases in Republican registration. However, in all three cities, Democratic Party registrations increased more than Republican Party registrations. Of the 1,167 voter registrations that the Republican Party lost, Oceanside accounted for 564

---

[160] Public Opinion Strategies: "Key Findings—California CD 49." September 9th, 2016.

lost voters, followed by Encinitas with 340 lost voters. Of the 880 voter registrations that the Democratic Party gained, Carlsbad accounted for 386 gained voters, followed by San Clemente with 173 voters. Within the district, Encinitas had the highest proportion of voters registered with the Democratic Party, at 38.1%, and San Clemente had the highest proportion of voters registered with the Republican Party, at 49.1%. Democrats were winning on Republican's home turf, and Republicans were losing on Democrat's home turf.

Nationally, partisan trends were moving in the opposite direction of the 49th Congressional District. Although the Republican registration advantage declined between May and September in the 49th Congressional District, the nationwide generic ballot showed Republicans catching up with Democrats. The NBC News/Wall Street Journal Survey found 45% of respondents preferred a Republican-controlled Congress in September, which was up from 44% in May. By comparison, 48% of respondents preferred a Democrat-controlled Congress in September, which was the same number as in May.[161]

---

[161] NBC News/Wall Street Journal Survey. Study #16804. Date Range: September 16th-19th, 2016.

In an attempt to appear more bipartisan, Congressman Issa endorsed Democrat Congresswoman Loretta Sanchez in her campaign to become the U.S. Senator from California. She was campaigning against Democrat Attorney General Kamala Harris. In an interview with the *Los Angeles Times*, Congressman Issa said, "I've already long ago figured out that Loretta Sanchez, her work on national security, probably tips the scale for a lot of us. She's also very well aware of our problems with water. So those are, in my particular case, making a difference that is pretty measurable."[162] The *Orange County Register* reported, "The Sanchez campaign is emphasizing her reputation as a moderate who can work with Republicans, as she tries to woo voters from both parties. Many [Republican] lawmakers consider [Attorney General Kamala] Harris a steadfast partisan and that's helped Sanchez win endorsements from several other prominent Republicans."[163] The *Los Angeles Times* published two letters to the editor that week related to Congressman Issa's endorsement of Congresswoman Loretta

---

[162] Willon, Phil. "One of California's Best-Known Republicans is Backing Democrat Loretta Sanchez for Senate." *Los Angeles Times*. September 3rd, 2016.

[163] Wisckol, Martin. "Issa Endorsements of Sanchez, Trump Bring Political Jiu Jitsu to House Race." *Orange County Register*. September 9th, 2016.

Sanchez. One stated: "The fact that a climate-change-denying ultraconservative such as Darrell Issa, who doesn't seem to mind spending taxpayer dollars so long as it's to conduct yet another pointless investigation of everything that the Obama administration does, is endorsing Loretta Sanchez [...] should be ample reason to vote for Kamala Harris." Another reader indicated Congressman Issa's endorsement caused him to regret having ever supported Congresswoman Loretta Sanchez.[164] On September 12th, Applegate for Congress distributed a press release stating Attorney General Kamala Harris had endorsed Colonel Applegate, calling him "The leader California needs in the House of Representatives." In the same press release, Colonel Applegate endorsed Attorney General Kamala Harris for the U.S. Senate.[165] Even though it was generally accepted that the congressional race would be determined by independents and disaffected Republicans, only Congressman Issa moved to appeal to voters not in his party, whereas Colonel Applegate presented himself as a partisan Democrat.

---

[164] *Los Angeles Times*. Letters to the Editor, September 8th, 2016.
[165] Applegate for Congress Press Release: "Attorney General Harris Calls Doug Applegate 'The Leader We Need in Congress.'" September 12th, 2016.

On September 13th, Politico reported, "Court records [...] show that [Colonel Applegate] in 2000 was charged with driving under the influence and pled guilty to reckless driving, then was ordered to attend a[n] alcohol abuse program. In 2004, Applegate was also ordered by the California Superior Court to surrender two firearms related to the domestic violence accusations made by his then-wife."[166] Shortly after the story broke, the National Republican Congressional Committee sent an email to its supporters highlighting the story, attempting to undermine Colonel Applegate's stance on women's issues. The *San Diego Union-Tribune* also reported on the Politico story and the National Republican Congressional Committee email. The article also featured an endorsement from Colonel Applegate's ex-wife and highlighted Congressman Issa's numerous run-ins with the law.[167]

The grand opening of the South Orange County Republican Headquarters was on September 16th. The new headquarters was within the boundaries of the 49th Congressional District.

---

[166] Marinucci, Carla. "Issa Challenger was Accused of 'Stalking,' Harassing Wife." Politico. September 13th, 2016.
[167] Stewart, Joshua. "Issa Challenger Faced Restraining Orders Related to Ex-Wife." *San Diego Union-Tribune*. September 13th, 2016.

Activists at that office had 53 calendar days to drive higher Republican turnout to push Congressman Issa, as well as other candidates, across the finish line on Election Day. Nationally, Reuters/Ipsos polled 1,489 registered voters, between September 8th and 12th, and found that 43% of respondents planned to vote for Democrat congressional candidates, whereas only 36% of respondents planned to vote for Republican congressional candidates.[168]   An Economist/YouGov poll of 1,085 registered voters between September 10th and 13th found that 44% of respondents planned to vote for Democrat congressional candidates, whereas only 38% planned to vote for Republican congressional candidates.[169]   Combined, these polls indicate Democrats had a 6.5-point lead on the generic ballot.

Both candidates launched television ads in the second-half of September, with the Applegate campaign releasing theirs first. The video released by Applegate for Congress was more anti-Issa than pro-Applegate.   It was titled "Lined Pockets," and attempted to link Congressman Issa to Donald Trump. The video showed a clip of Donald Trump

---

[168] Reuters/Ipsos. "Core Political Data." Published September 13th, 2016.

[169] Economist/YouGov Poll, conducted September 10th-13th, 2016.

saying "I'm very rich," and "Nobody knows the system better than me." A voiceover then says, "Just like Trump, Issa gamed the system to line his own pockets, steering millions in taxpayer money to help properties he owned. Issa's wealth increased to over two hundred fifty million dollars during his time in Congress." The background of the video alludes to a 2011 *New York Times* investigation about Congressman Issa's amendments in spending bills related to his own assets in California. The video ends with Colonel Applegate saying, "It's time we had a Congressman who looks out for you not himself. I'm Colonel Doug Applegate and I approve this message because I'll always fight for you."[170]

As the political ad was airing, another difference between the candidates' focuses emerged. While Colonel Applegate attempted to make the contest in the 49th Congressional District about Donald Trump, Congressman Issa continued to focus on local issues. The day after Applegate for Congress released the television ad, Issa for Congress announced that San Diego County Sheriff Bill Gore and Orange County Sheriff Sandra Hutchens had endorsed Congressman Issa for re-election. The

---

[170] Applegate for Congress Press Release: "Applegate Campaign Hits Issa in First TV Ad." September 21st, 2016.

Orange County Board of Supervisors had appointed Sheriff Sandra Hutchens in 2008, after the previous sheriff had been federally indicted for public corruption charges.[171] The San Diego County Board of Supervisors had appointed Sheriff Bill Gore in 2009, after the previous sheriff had announced his retirement.[172] Both of them received more than fifty percent of the vote in three-candidate races when they ran for re-election in 2010. Both of them ran un-opposed in 2014.[173] Neither of their offices were up for re-election in 2016. Although county sheriffs are elected, the races are officially non-partisan. Again, we see that Colonel Applegate was attempting to make the race a partisan contest focused on national politics, whereas Congressman Issa was focused on bi-partisan or non-partisan local issues.

Issa for Congress released two television ads in the next week. One of them was pro-Issa and the other was anti-Applegate. Issa for Congress also launched the website colonelapplegate.com, which portrayed Colonel Applegate as "another left-wing extremist California just can't afford." An article in

---

[171] Lowe, Peggy. "Sandra Hutchens Publicly Sworn in as Sheriff." *Orange County Register*. June 24th, 2008.
[172] McDonald, Jeff. "Supervisors Appoint Gore Sheriff." *San Diego Union-Tribune*. June 16th, 2009.
[173] Orange County and San Diego County Registrar of Voters information for 2010 and 2014.

the *Orange County Register* stated Congressman Issa's attacks on Colonel Applegate were "the latest sign that the Vista Republican has a reelection battle on his hands for the first time since winning office in 2000." The article also noted that it is rare for incumbents to attack challengers, which costs money, unless the race is close. Jodi Balma, a political scientist at Fullerton College, was quoted as saying, "Many of Applegate's votes are anti-Issa. They don't know Applegate, so Issa is trying to throw doubt on who he is."[174]

One of the television ads from Issa for Congress was titled "Our Congressman." A United States Marine Corps veteran and his wife shared a story about Congressman Issa helping them resolve an issue receiving benefits from Veterans Affairs. Another woman with a daughter in the United States Army shared a story about her daughter writing a letter to Congressman Issa, who then wrote back to encourage her to be in public service. Lastly, a recent college graduate said she wanted Congressman Issa to stay in Congress to promote the sharing economy. The other television ad from Issa for Congress was titled "Litmus Test." The ad associated Colonel Applegate with Congresswoman Nancy Pelosi, the

---

[174] Wiskhol, Martin. "Congressman Darrell Issa Attacks Campaign Foe Doug Applegate in Sign that Race is Competitive." *Orange County Register*. September 29th, 2016.

House Minority Leader at the time. It stated Colonel Applegate supported higher business taxes, a carbon tax, and a government takeover of the healthcare system. The ad ends with the line: "Nancy Pelosi picked him, but we can't afford him!" Both ads first aired on television during the first presidential debate between Hillary Clinton and Donald Trump on September 26th.[175]

In the first round of political ads in the campaign, Issa for Congress seems to have been more effective than Applegate for Congress. The 2011 *New York Times* investigation was unlikely to be a determining factor in the 2016 election, considering the fact that Congressman Issa had already won two elections within the new boundaries of the district since the article was published. Republicans or independent voters that leaned Republican were unlikely to be swayed by an anti-Issa article from the *New York Times* due to the organization's partisan nature. The last Republican candidate for president to be endorsed by the *New York Times* was Dwight D. Eisenhower, in 1956.[176] However, an undecided voter

---

[175] Issa for Congress Press Release: "Issa Announces 2 New TV Spots Highlighting Work for Community and Opponent's Extreme Agenda." September 26th, 2016.

[176] The Editorial Board. "*New York Times* Endorsements Through the Ages." *New York Times*. September 23rd, 2016.

might not have known of Colonel Applegate's viewpoints. With the first ads, Colonel Applegate's views were presented to undecided voters on terms set by the Issa campaign. The first ad from the Issa campaign also highlighted his work towards two of the largest institutions in his district: Marine Corps Base Camp Pendleton and the University of California, San Diego. Both of these would help with independent voters. The second ad from the Issa campaign also helped re-enforce the need for Republicans in the district to go to the polls on Election Day, regardless of their views towards Donald Trump. California Republicans most likely could not stop Hillary Clinton from taking the White House, but they still could likely stop Congresswoman Nancy Pelosi from controlling the House of Representatives. A Reuters/Ipsos poll of 1,457 registered voters between September 15th and 19th found that 43% of respondents favored Democrat congressional candidates, whereas only 35% of respondents favored Republican congressional candidates. Interestingly, among 1,111 likely voters, the same poll found respondents favored Republicans 40% to 39%.[177] The expectation that Hillary Clinton

---

[177] Reuters/Ipsos. "Core Political Data." Published September 20th, 2016.

would win the presidency might have driven more Republican support for congressional candidates, both nationwide and in the 49th Congressional District.

A lawyer for Issa for Congress sent a letter to Applegate for Congress stating the "Lined Pockets" advertisement "contains false information deliberately and knowingly intended to mislead California voters and defame Congressman Issa's reputation." The primary issue was that the advertisement depicted a *New York Times* article dated August 14th, 2011, with the quote: "Rep. Issa gamed the system to line his own pockets. Steering millions in taxpayer money to help properties he owns." The lawyer claimed: "Viewers are clearly led to believe that the statement with quotation marks is a quote from an article in the *New York Times*. Yet, as a simple review of the articles reflects, the words in quotation marks do not appear anywhere in the referenced article (or any other news article, for that matter)." The letter determined this would constitute "actual malice" as was used in the case of *New York Times Co. v. Sullivan*, 376 U.S. 254 (1964).[178]

---

[178] Letter dated September 29th, 2016 from J. Randy Evans of Dentons US LLP, addressed to Colonel Doug Applegate and Robert Dempsey.

In late September, the *Orange County Register* reported on Republican Party activists' attempts to drive turnout for down-ballot races despite low enthusiasm for Donald Trump in California. The article noted that California State Senate Republican candidate Assemblywoman Ling Ling Chang had distanced herself from Donald Trump, whereas "a key strategy of local Democratic congressional candidate Doug Applegate's campaign is reminding voters that his opponent, Rep. Darrell Issa, has endorsed Trump." The article was primarily about a national political action committee called Republicans for Clinton '16, which was "actively campaigning to both defeat Trump and maintain Republican majorities in the House and Senate." The concern among some Republicans was that President Trump would divide the Republican Party, whereas a so-called third term of President Obama would unite Republicans. When the article was published, 34 Republican staffers and elected officials had endorsed Republicans for Clinton '16, which was founded by two members of the George W. Bush Administration.[179] The article did not mention that in the primary, Congressman Issa had received more

---

[179] Wisckol, Martin. "'Republicans for Clinton' Back Down-Ticket GOP Candidates." *Orange County Register*. September 23rd, 2016.

votes than candidate Donald Trump. Congressman Issa had already won an election with low Republican approval for Donald Trump, and nothing indicated that would change in the general election. Additionally, each time the media doubted Donald Trump's chances of winning the presidency, Republicans had even more incentive to turn out for congressional candidates to maintain the balance of power in the federal government.

In the month of September, voter registrations in the portion of the 49th Congressional District in San Diego County dropped by 3,409 voters since the prior month's registration report. Both Republican Party and Democratic Party registrations declined, but Republican Party registrations declined twice as fast as Democratic Party registrations. The Republican Party voter registration advantage in that part of the district declined from 8,239 voters at the end of August to 6,858 voters at the end of September, a 16.7% decline in one month.[180] At the end of September, the Rothenberg & Gonzales Political Report reclassified the 49th Congressional District from "Safe Republican" to "Republican Favored."[181]

---

[180] San Diego County Registrar of Voters. "Report of Registration – State Reporting Districts." October 3rd, 2016.
[181] Gonzales, Nathan. "GOP House Majority Still Solid...For Now." Inside Elections. September 30th, 2016.

Tulchin Research conducted a poll at the end of September and claimed 46% of voters supported Doug Applegate, 42% of voters supported Darrell Issa, and 12% of voters were undecided. The margin of error was reported to be 4.9%.[182] This was the first poll to show that Colonel Applegate was leading Congressman Issa.

By the end of the third quarter of 2016, the Issa campaign had raised $1.4 million, spent $2.2 million, and had $3.0 million cash on hand.[183] At least $535,000 was spent on mailings, yard signs, bumper stickers, and shirts during the quarter. The largest single expense was a $303,000 media buy, followed by $187,000 online advertising costs. The campaign spent $107,000 on campaign consulting, $30,000 on strategic consulting, and $18,000 on fundraising consulting. The campaign also hired a field campaign director and at least twenty paid canvassers.[184] Pictures tweeted by the Issa campaign on September 22nd and 23rd show at least 30 volunteers working for the campaign. The Applegate campaign had

---

[182] Tulchin Research: "California Congressional District 49: Polling Finds Real Opportunity for Democratic Pickup as Applegate Now Leads Issa." October 3rd, 2016.
[183] Filing FEC-1108570. Form 3: October Quarterly. Filed October 15th, 2016.
[184] Filing FEC-1108570. Schedule B. Filed October 15th, 2016.

raised $779,000, spent $623,000, and had $161,000 cash on hand.[185]

Throughout September, the Issa campaign and the local Republican Party were focused on campaigning much more than in previous years, but that did not seem to reverse the district's trend towards the Democratic Party. The registration advantage was still declining, election forecasters were downgrading Congressman Issa's chances, and recent polling was showing Colonel Applegate ahead. The Issa campaign only had a few weeks to turn it around.

---

[185] Filing FEC-1151822. Form 3: October Quarterly. Amendment 1. Filed March 9th, 2017.

CHAPTER 7: OCTOBER – ONE MONTH UNTIL THE GENERAL ELECTION

Congressman Issa began October with endorsements from two prominent business organizations. The U.S. Chamber of Commerce, which at that time represented over three million businesses, endorsed Congressman Issa, and stated his record in Congress had earned a score of 93% from the organization. The National Federation of Independent Businesses also endorsed Congressman Issa, stating: "On every critical vote this Congress, he stood with small business owners."[186] Although Issa for Congress presented these organizations as "jobs groups," they are both pro-Republican groups. In the 2014 election, less than one percent of contributions

---

[186] Issa for Congress Press Release: "Jobs Groups Endorse Congressman Darrell Issa." October 3rd, 2016.

from the U.S. Chamber of Commerce went to Democrat U.S. House of Representative candidates. In the same election cycle, about four percent of contributions from the National Federation of Independent Businesses went to Democrat House candidates.[187] However, most people did not know this, and these endorsements followed an endorsement from the San Diego Regional Chamber of Commerce in July. That group had endorsed candidates from both major parties.

Within the district, Congressman Issa, State Senator Pat Bates, Assemblyman Rocky Chavez, and Oceanside Councilman Jerry Kern held a forum in Oceanside on sober living homes on Monday, October 3rd. At the beginning of the previous month, a similar forum was held in San Clemente, attracting 300 participants. This forum was reported as having 100 attendees.[188] In an election determined by 1,600 votes, these two forums allowed Congressman Issa to reach between 200 and 400 people passionate enough about this one issue to attend a meeting about it. If each of them convinced their spouse, their neighbor, or their colleagues to vote for Congressman Issa due

---

[187] Center for Responsive Politics (OpenSecrets.org) data.
[188] Sifuentes, Edward. "Officials Hold Town Hall to Address Sober-Living Homes." *San Diego Union-Tribune*. October 3rd, 2016.

to his work on sober living homes, these two forums might have pushed Congressman Issa over the finish line.

The *San Diego Union-Tribune* published articles on two consecutive days about the political ads released in September. The first article compared the tone of the television ads in the 49th Congressional District and the 52nd Congressional District, which is also along the coast in San Diego County. The article implied that Congressman Issa first released an ad that, "paints his opponent, Democrat Doug Applegate, as a left-wing extremist." Colonel Applegate is portrayed as responding to Congressman Issa's ad "by linking him to GOP presidential nominee Donald Trump and highlighting a report that he has personally benefited from his actions in Washington." Actually, Colonel Applegate had been the first to release an attack ad. By comparison to the television ads in the 49th Congressional District, candidates in the 52nd Congressional District are "comparatively upbeat, with neither airing attack ads. The candidates are smiling, in casual clothes, and talk about how they think they can help out constituents."[189] A second

---

[189] Stewart, Joshua. "Two Big Congressional Races Start TV Ad Campaigns." *San Diego Union-Tribune.* October 3rd, 2016.

article reported Congressman Issa's threat to sue Colonel Applegate over the television ad based on the 2011 *New York Times* investigation into Congressman Issa's earmarks and personal property. The article gave the opportunity for Colonel Applegate to both remind readers of his own combat experience and Congressman Issa's partisanship in Congress. Colonel Applegate was quoted as saying, "I'm a Marine Colonel who volunteered to go to Iraq in 2006 and spent a good chunk of my tour in Ramadi. Congressman Issa's money and lawyers don't scare me one bit. It's incredible that someone whose career consists of conducting costly, partisan investigations is so thin-skinned."[190]

On October 4th, the Applegate campaign released a television commercial titled "Everything Changed." The ad shows images from the September 11th Attack on New York City. It is narrated by a first responder, who says: "Things changed that day. Nobody got out unscathed. Then, Darrell Issa and the Tea Party Republicans tried to play politics with our lives. The Tea Party Republicans actually voted to deny healthcare to 9/11 first responders. Issa said he had done enough for something that was simply a

---

[190] Stewart, Joshua. "Issa Challenges Applegate's Attack Ads." *San Diego Union-Tribune.* October 4th, 2016.

plane crash. Darrell Issa and the Tea Party Republicans, they turned their backs on all of us."

In a press release, the Applegate campaign claimed Congressman Issa refused to vote on a first responder healthcare bill, referring to H.R. 2926 Air Transportation Safety and System Stabilization Act.[191] However, the bill passed the House of Representatives with more Republican support than Democrat support. Only six Republicans voted against the bill, one of them being Congressman Ron "Dr. No" Paul from Texas, whereas 46 Democrats voted against the bill. Congressman Issa did not vote for or against the bill. The attack ad also referenced H.R. 847 James Zadroga 9/11 Health and Compensation Act. Eric Cantor, John Boehner, Paul Ryan, Michele Bachmann, Jason Chaffetz, and Steve Scalise are shown in the ad voting against the act, which they did on September 29th, 2010. However, the House of Representatives voted on a revised bill on December 22nd, 2010. Jason Chaffetz and 30 other Republicans voted for it. John Boehner, Paul Ryan, Darrell Issa, 86 other Republicans, and 79 Democrats did not vote for or against the bill. It passed and

---

[191] Applegate for Congress Press Release: "First Responder: Issa's Lip Service is Disgraceful." October 6th, 2016.

President Obama signed it into law on January 2nd, 2011.

A similar bill, H.R. 2029, was voted on in 2015. Darrell Issa, Paul Ryan, and Jason Chaffetz all voted for the bill. (The other "Tea Party Republicans" mentioned in the ad were no longer in Congress by that time.)

For Colonel Applegate, this was a very odd issue on which to attack Congressman Issa. Congressman Issa has been re-elected seven times since he did not vote on the original bill in 2001. Congressman Issa has been re-elected three times since he voted against the first version of the 2010 bill. Neither of these votes were ever issues for voters in the past.

Public Opinion Strategies conducted another poll on behalf of the Issa campaign between October 4th and 6th. This poll indicated 48% of voters supported Congressman Issa, 39% of voters supported Colonel Applegate, and 13% of voters were undecided. The margin of error was reported to be 4.9%.[192]   Since Public Opinion Strategies last conducted a poll for the Issa campaign in early September, support for Congressman Issa had

---

[192] Public Opinion Strategies: "Key Findings—California CD 49." October 11th, 2016.

dropped from 52% to 48% and support for Colonel Applegate had risen from 38% to 39%. Regardless of the accuracy of Colonel Applegate's attacks on Congressman Issa, they seemed to be moving public opinion in the direction he desired.

Despite Colonel Applegate focusing his other attacks on Congressman Issa's relationship with Donald Trump, Congressman Issa furthered the relationship. On October 7th, the Trump campaign added Congressman Issa, as well as four Republican senators, one Republican congressman, and others, to its National Security Advisory Council.[193] That same day, the *Washington Post* published an Access Hollywood video from 2005, where Donald Trump was arriving on the set of "Days of Our Lives." Donald Trump was recorded saying: "I moved on her like a bitch, but I couldn't get there. And she was married. Then all of a sudden I see her, she's now got the big phony tits and everything. She's totally changed her look." After he noticed the actress that would escort them to the set, he said, "I've got to use some Tic Tacs, just in case I start kissing her. You know I'm automatically attracted to beautiful—I just start kissing them. It's like a magnet. Just kiss. I don't

---

[193] Wallbank, Derek. "Trump Campaign Adds to National Security Advisory Council." Bloomberg L.P. October 7th, 2016.

even wait. And when you're a star, they let you do it. You can do anything. ... Grab them by the pussy. You can do anything."[194]

Congressman Issa linked to the original *Washington Post* article on Facebook and stated, "This type of behavior has no place in American politics, especially not from those seeking to lead our great nation."   The *Los Angeles Times* noted that Congressman Issa, as well as a few other California Republicans, had criticized Donald Trump immediately after the video was released, but had not rescinded their endorsements.[195]

The second presidential debate between Donald Trump and Hillary Clinton occurred on Sunday, October 9th, two days after the *Washington Post* article. Immediately before the debate, Donald Trump held a surprise press conference with Paula Jones, Kathleen Willey, Juanita Broaddrick, and Kathy Shelton. In 1998, President Clinton agreed to pay Paula Jones $850,000 to settle a sexual harassment

---

[194] Fahrenthold, David. "Trump Recorded Having Extremely Lewd Conversation About Women in 2005." *Washington Post.* October 8th, 2016.

[195] Wire, Sarah. "Darrell Issa is Among the California Republicans Who have Criticized Trump but haven't Rescinded Their Endorsements." *Los Angeles Times*. October 8th, 2016.

lawsuit out of court.[196] Kathleen Willey, during an interview with 60 Minutes on March 15th, 1998, accused President Clinton of inappropriate touching.[197] Juanita Broaddrick, during an interview with Dateline on February 24, 1999, stated that Bill Clinton had raped her in 1978, when he was the Arkansas Attorney General.[198] Thomas Alfred Taylor was accused of raping Kathy Shelton, who at the time was twelve years old, on May 10, 1975. The charges were punishable by 30 years to life in prison. Hillary Rodham, later Hillary Rodham Clinton, was the defendant's attorney. Due to procedural errors, the defendant was only sentenced to five years in prison for a lesser charge, but given credit for time already spent in county jail.[199] A scandal that should have sunk Donald Trump's candidacy was used to highlight Bill and Hillary Clinton's handling of sexual assault and rape allocations in the past.

The next day, on October 10th, the Issa campaign also jumped on the opportunity to highlight the comments Colonel Applegate's ex-wife

---

[196] Baker, Peter. "Clinton Settles Paula Jones Lawsuit for $850,000." *Washington Post*. November 14th, 1998.

[197] CBS News: 60 Minutes with Ed Bradley. Aired March 15th, 1998.

[198] NBC News: Dateline with Lisa Myers. Aired February 24th, 1999.

[199] *State of Arkansas v. Thomas Alfred Taylor*, CR 75-203.

made about him during their divorce. The Issa campaign released a television commercial titled "Dangerous," which was the word Colonel Applegate's ex-wife had used to describe his "obsession" with her and her new spouse. Calvin Moore, the Issa campaign spokesman, said, "Democrats concerned about Donald Trump's behavior and temperament should be all-the-more concerned about Doug Applegate's. The hair-raising details in these court records speak volumes to his character, unstable temperament and treatment of women which make it clear he's just not fit to serve us in Congress."[200] Not only did Donald Trump use the opportunity to put the Clintons on defense, Congressman Issa used the opportunity to put Colonel Applegate on defense.

Reuters/Ipsos surveys from before and after the Access Hollywood tape and the second presidential debate can be compared to measure these events' impact on voters. Reuters/Ipsos polled 1,669 registered voters and 1,239 likely voters between September 29th and October 3rd, which can be used as a baseline for sentiment before these two events.[201]

---

[200] Issa for Congress Press Release: "Issa Campaign Releases New TV Ad: 'Dangerous.'" October 10th, 2016.
[201] Reuters/Ipsos. "Core Political Data." Published October 4th, 2016.

Reuters/Ipsos also polled 1,501 registered voters and 1,190 likely voters between October 13th and October 17th, which can be used to understand the change in sentiment from the survey before these two events.[202] Hillary Clinton remained flat with likely voters, but dropped in support among registered voters, from 44% to 42%. Donald Trump grew his support among likely voters from 36% to 38% and also grew his support among registered voters from 33% to 34%. Democrats gained one point among both likely voters and registered voters on the generic ballot. Republicans gained one point among likely voters, and remained flat at 35% among registered voters. According to Reuters/Ipsos, Donald Trump managed to come out of the Access Hollywood ordeal better than Hillary Clinton did overall, and Republican congressional candidates were no worse off than they were before, among likely voters.

Immediately following the "Dangerous" ad, the Issa campaign released a television ad titled "No Greater Champion," featuring Rudy Giuliani, the Republican Mayor of New York City from 1994 to 2001. The entire ad consisted of Mayor Giuliani looking at the camera and saying: "After the terrorist

---

[202] Reuters/Ipsos. "Core Political Data." Published October 18th, 2016.

attack of September 11th, our country came together like no other time in our history. Congressman Darrell Issa was one of the people I turned to for help. That's why I was so shocked and angry to hear that his opponent was falsely attacking Darrell and using images of September 11th to do it! Doug Applegate should be ashamed of himself. Law enforcement and first responders have no greater champion in Congress than Darrell Issa and I'm proud to support him."[203]

There are two significant aspects of Rudy Giuliani's endorsement of Congressman Issa. First, it directly countered the Applegate campaign's criticisms of Congressman Issa's voting record related to the September 11th Attack. Second, it indicated a continued relationship with the Trump campaign. Politico reported that after the Access Hollywood video surfaced, "Trump had hunkered down on Sunday morning, including pulling back top aides from planned national appearances," and "Only Rudy Giuliani was dispatched to inject the Trump campaign's position into the national conversation during a round of Sunday morning news shows."[204]

---

[203] Issa for Congress Press Release: "Issa Releases New Ad Featuring Rudy Giuliani." October 11th, 2016.
[204] Cheney, Kyle and Goldmacher, Shane. "Trump Launches Sneak Attack Ahead of Debate." Politico. October 9th, 2016.

Rudy Giuliani had been the face of the Trump campaign during a crisis, and now was brought in to defend Congressman Issa.

One day after the Issa campaign released the ad with Rudy Giuliani, the Applegate campaign released an ad titled "Access." The ad showed pictures of Congressman Issa shaking hands with Donald Trump between censored clips of Donald Trump's comments in the Access Hollywood video. The narrator made the statement: "On the day we saw the real Donald Trump, Darrell Issa decided to join Trump's campaign." While technically true, Congressman Issa joined the National Security Advisory Council before the Access Hollywood video was published. The video called on voters to "Say no to Donald Trump and Darrell Issa."[205]

On October 13th, the Issa campaign released videos of Colonel Applegate implying to the audience at an Energy Upgrade California forum during the previous weekend that he was not being fully honest with voters. He said, "I've been a trial lawyer for three and a half decades, I don't usually lead with that because I'm not going to get any votes by being an attorney. But this is a different crowd so I'm going

---

[205] Applegate for Congress Press Release: "Colonel Applegate's New Ad: Say No to Trump and Issa." October 11th, 2016.

to be a little bit more honest. […] I wish I could talk in detail. They sort of don't let you do that when you're in the middle of a campaign. They say stick to the elevator speech. Don't get outside your lane." The statement "I'm going to be a little bit more honest," was said in jest, but easily taken out of context, as it was by the Issa campaign. A likely more damaging statement that Colonel Applegate made was his response to a question about reaching across the aisle. He said, "First of all I think that's the wrong premise. I think we're past, if we were ever there, reaching across the aisle."[206] For Colonel Applegate to win, he needed Republicans to not show up to vote and un-affiliated voters to vote for him. However, his remarks at an event he felt he could be more honest showed that he had no intention of working with Republicans.

The Camp Pendleton Mainside Post Office was renamed the Camp Pendleton Medal of Honor Post Office in October due to legislation introduced by Congressman Issa. The *San Diego Union-Tribune* reported on the planned change one week before the

---

[206] Issa for Congress Press Release: "Applegate Shows His True Colors." October 13th, 2016.

ceremony.[207] On the day of the ceremony, the *Orange County Register* reported that Brig. Gen. Kevin J. Killea, commanding general of Marine Corps Installations West and Marine Corps Base Camp Pendleton, thanked Congressman Issa for introducing the legislation, which was signed into law by President Barack Obama on June 13th.[208] Although this event appeared to be a political stunt to limit Colonel Applegate's appeal with voters tied to Camp Pendleton, technically the bill was introduced in March, which was three months before the surprise result of the primary election.

The Federal Election Commission requires candidates to report on campaign finances up to October 19th in the Pre-General Report. Up to October 19th, Issa for Congress had raised $1.7 million, spent $3.9 million, and had $1.7 million cash on hand.[209] In the 19 calendar days between the end of the third quarter and October 19th, the campaign spent $966,000 on media buys. Printing and mailing cost at least $274,000. Campaign, get-out-the-vote,

---

[207] McIntosh, Linda. "Pendleton Post Office Named After Medal of Honor Recipients." *San Diego Union-Tribune*. October 11th, 2016.
[208] Ritchie, Erika. "Camp Pendleton Post Office salutes the Selfless." *Orange County Register*. October 18th, 2016.
[209] Filing FEC-1119424. Form 3: Pre-General. Filed October 27th, 2016.

fundraising, and strategy consulting services cost $105,000. Digital advertising cost $78,000. At least fifteen paid canvassers were walking precincts.[210] The Applegate campaign had raised $1.2 million, spent $1.0 million, and had $1.9 million cash on hand.[211] The campaign's largest expense, by far, was a $329,000 media buy. It spent $60,000 on digital and strategy consulting. At least nine people were on payroll.[212] For the first time, the Applegate campaign had more cash on hand than the Issa campaign.

As October drew to a close, Congressman Issa received endorsements from the two major local newspapers. On October 20th, the *Orange County Register* endorsed Congressman Issa. The Editorial Board noted that Congressman Issa was in his toughest re-election campaign so far, but found "no reason to unseat Issa, who has remained a consistent voice for fiscal responsibility and limited government during his time in our nation's capital." In regards to Congressman Issa's opponent, the Editorial Board said: "We found Doug Applegate's thoughts on foreign affairs, military engagement and his military

---

[210] Filing FEC-1119424. Schedule B. Filed October 27th, 2016.
[211] Filing FEC-1152780. Form 3: Pre-General. Filed March 17th, 2017.
[212] Filing FEC-1152780. Form 3: Schedule B. Filed March 17th, 2017.

service worthy of praise but, overall, we found Issa to be more agreeable on the majority of policy issues."[213] The Editorial Board also endorsed Democrat State Senator Lou Correa to replace Democrat Congresswoman Loretta Sanchez,[214] as well as endorsed Republican Congresswoman Mimi Walters,[215] Republican Congressman Ed Royce,[216] and Democrat Congresswoman Linda Sanchez[217] for re-election. On October 24th, the *San Diego Union-Tribune* endorsed Congressman Issa. Although the endorsement highlighted his partisanship as chairman of the House Oversight and Government Reform Committee, it also stated he had been "very constructive on lower profile issues." It stated Colonel Applegate "came across as deeply knowledgeable about foreign affairs." However, overall, the Editorial Board determined Congressman Issa was "more likely to be able to get things done for his district and California, especially with Republican

---

[213] The Editorial Board. "Re-Elect Darrell Issa to Congress." *Orange County Register*. October 20th, 2016.

[214] The Editorial Board. "Correa for Congress." *Orange County Register*. October 19th, 2016.

[215] The Editorial board. "Re-Elect Mimi Walters." *Orange County Register*. October 21st, 2016.

[216] The Editorial Board. "Re-Elect Ed Royce." *Orange County Register*. October 26th, 2016.

[217] The Editorial Board. "Re-elect Linda Sanchez." *Orange County Register*. October 27th, 2016.

control of the House seemingly likely until redistricting in 2022." Thus, the Editorial Board endorsed Congressman Issa for re-election.[218] On the same day, the *San Diego Union-Tribune* also endorsed Democrat Congressman Peters, noting "he's worked well on regional concerns with others in the San Diego County congressional delegation—not just Democrats but Republicans, including Darrell Issa, R-Vista, and Duncan Hunter, R-Alpine."[219] Prior to the 2016 election, the *San Diego Union-Tribune* had not endorsed a Democrat for president, but it endorsed Hillary Clinton on September 30th. The paper called her "the safe choice for the U.S. and for the world, for Democrats and Republicans alike."[220]

The *Los Angeles Times* did not make an endorsement in the 49th Congressional District. However, the paper's Editorial Board issued a blanket denunciation of the California Republican Party, even questioning the merits of a two-party system in California. A two-party system "works for the public only when there are two responsible parties participating." In the opinion of the Editorial Board,

---

[218] The Editorial Board. "Why Rep. Darrell Issa Deserves to be Re-Elected." *San Diego Union-Tribune.* October 24th, 2016.
[219] The Editorial Board. "Rep. Scott Peters Has Earned Third Term in House." *San Diego Union-Tribune.* October 24th, 2016.
[220] The Editorial Board. "Why Hillary Clinton is the Safe Choice for President." *San Diego Union-Tribune.* September 30th, 2016.

"The state's GOP has ceased to be responsible."[221] The *Los Angeles Times* did report that President Obama had endorsed Colonel Applegate, as well as two other Democrat congressional candidates challenging incumbent Republicans in California's 10th and 25th Congressional Districts.[222] In 2012, President Obama won the 10th Congressional District with 50.6% of the vote, lost the 25th Congressional District with only 47.8% of the vote, and lost the 49th Congressional District with only 45.7% of the vote.[223]

The voter registration deadline for the general election was October 24th. Between the registration close date for the primary election and the registration close date for the general election, total voter registrations in the 49th Congressional District increased by 28,790 voters. Registrations not aligned with either major party increased by 15,371 voters. Democratic Party registrations increased more than twice as fast as Republican Party registrations; 9,138 net new Democrats to 4,281 net new Republicans.

---

[221] The Editorial Board. "California's shrinking GOP." *Los Angeles Times*. October 20th, 2016.

[222] Mai-Duc, Christine. "Here are the California Democrats President Obama has not Endorsed for Congress." *Los Angeles Times*. October 24th, 2016.

[223] California Secretary of State: 2012 General Election Statement of the Vote: Counties by Congressional Districts for President.

The Republican registration advantage in the 49th Congressional District had declined to 25,000 voters.

Although the 49th Congressional District was formed in 2011, information for the nine cities within the district can be collected for 2008. The 2008 election was the last election an incumbent president was not running. Voter registrations in those nine cities accounted for more than 85% of total voter registrations in the district as of October 24th, 2016. Between the general election in 2008 and 2016, total voter registrations increased by 28,357 voters in those nine cities. Registrations not affiliated with either major party increased the most, at 21,355 net voters. Registrations affiliated with the Democratic Party increased 13,221 net voters, whereas registrations affiliated with the Republican Party decreased 6,219 net voters. The Republican voter registration advantage in those nine cities had dropped from over 38,000 in 2008 to only 18,000 in 2016. Even though Republicans still outnumbered Democrats in the 49th Congressional District, the Democratic Party had more momentum going into the election. The voter registration situation for the Republican Party would have been even worse had the Issa campaign not had voter registration drives at the Oceanside Sunset Market on September 30th and the Encinitas Oktoberfest on October 2nd.

On October 22nd, the San Diego County Democratic Party sent out a media advisory stating: "House Democratic Leader Nancy Pelosi will join the San Diego County Democratic Party and top local Democratic leaders on Monday to urge women to vote to keep Donald Trump out of the White House, to send Reps. Scott Peters and Susan Davis back to Congress, and to help Colonel Doug Applegate defeat Darrell Issa." The event was to be held two days later, on a Monday, at the San Diego Democratic Coordinated Campaign Office, which is not within the boundaries of the 49th Congressional District, and jointly organized with Planned Parenthood.[224] During the event, Congresswoman Pelosi was quoted saying "Hillary Clinton's victory is such a foregone conclusion that maybe people might not turn out to vote," but pleaded with activists to get out the vote because "A big vote for Hillary Clinton is the best antidote for the poison the Republicans are spewing." Congresswoman Davis predicted the Democrats would flip about 20 seats in the House of Representatives, which would not still not give Democrats a majority. Congressman Peters was quoted saying: "It's time to give President Clinton a

---

[224] San Diego County Democratic Party Press Release: "Nancy Pelosi to Rally Volunteers to Turn Out Women Voters." October 22nd, 2016.

Congress she can work with."[225] At about that time, Reuters/Ipsos polled 1,170 likely voters, and found that 44% of respondents planned to vote for a Democrat congressional candidate, whereas only 39% of respondents planned to vote for a Republican congressional candidate. Among 1,506 registered voters, 45% of respondents planned to vote for a Democrat congressional candidate, whereas only 37% planned to vote for a Republican congressional candidate.[226] That gave Democrats a 5-point lead among likely voters, and an 8-point lead among registered voters. An Economist/YouGov poll of 1,376 registered voters at about the same time found that 43% of respondents planned to vote for a Democrat congressional candidate, whereas only 39% of respondents planned to vote for a Republican congressional candidate. Interestingly, when those same respondents were asked which party they prefer controls Congress, 42% preferred a Republican-controlled Congress, whereas only 40% preferred a Democrat-controlled Congress.[227] Voters seemed to

---

[225] Jennewein, Chris. "Nancy Pelosi Sees Hillary Clinton Victory—If Voters Turn Out." *Times of San Diego*. October 24th, 2016.

[226] Reuters/Ipsos. "Core Political Data." Published October 25th, 2016.

[227] Economist/YouGov Poll, conducted October 22nd-26th, 2016.

favor Democrat candidates, but at the same time also favor divided government.

Just as Congressman Issa had not distanced himself from Donald Trump after the Applegate campaign attacked the relationship, Colonel Applegate also did not distance himself from Congresswoman Pelosi after the Issa campaign attacked the relationship. If Secretary Clinton's victory was inevitable, incumbent Republican senators in Illinois, Wisconsin, Pennsylvania, and New Hampshire would also likely lose. That would bring the number of Republicans in the U.S. Senate down from 54 to 50, out of 100 senators. Tie votes in the U.S. Senate would be broken by the vice president. Although the goal of Congresswoman Pelosi's visit was to drive Democrat turnout in San Diego County, it also served as a reminder to local Republican activists that the only way to maintain control over at least one branch of government was to re-elect more Republican incumbents in the House of Representatives. That likely mobilized more votes for Congressman Issa.

President Obama attended a fundraiser in La Jolla on the night of October 23rd. La Jolla is a community just south of the 49th Congressional District's boundary. In the prior week, the Issa Campaign had sent out a mailer with a picture of

President Obama at his desk with a pen in hand. A quote from Congressman Issa appears next to President Obama saying: "I am very pleased that President Obama has signed into law the Survivor's Bill of Rights—legislation I co-sponsored to protect the victims of sexual assault." Congressman Issa does not identify himself as a Republican in the mailer.

At the fundraiser, President Obama was quoted as saying, "Issa's primary contribution to the United States Congress has been to obstruct and to waste taxpayer dollars on trumped-up investigations that have led nowhere." He called the mailer "the definition of chutzpah," and later in the night added that it was "shameless." President Obama also claimed during the event that he had not had a major scandal in his administration.[228]

Congressman Issa was interviewed by Fox News the next day to discuss his reaction to President Obama's comments. Congressman Issa spent much of the interview supporting his claim that he was able to work with the president on many issues, despite being chairman of the House Oversight Committee. He mentioned that the president had signed 23 bills that had gone through the Oversight Committee, as

---

[228] Eilperin, Juliet. "Obama: Issa Making a 'Shameless' Attempt to Portray Himself as an Ally." *Washington Post.* October 24th, 2016.

well as his time working with Vice President Joe Biden on expansion of the Violence Against Women Act. Immediately before the interview, Congressman Issa had voted with the president, and against the majority of Republicans, on a bill that would have allowed 9/11 victims' families to sue Saudi Arabia. The last point he made in the interview was about American's desire for accountability in government. Neil Cavuto, the host of the show, indicated Fox News had attempted to contact Colonel Applegate, but had not heard back.[229] If true, the Applegate campaign missed a chance to directly address Republican voters and conservative independents.

Two revelations that week provided Congressman Issa with the opportunity to reply directly on a national stage to President Obama's assertion of maintaining a scandal-free administration. The first revelation came on October 25th via WikiLeaks. A hacked email written in 2015 to John Podesta and others showed that multiple associates of Hillary Clinton were concerned by President Obama's statement that he had heard about Hillary Clinton's private email from news reports. Cheryl Mills, an aide to Hillary Clinton, replied to the

---

[229] Fox News: Your World with Neil Cavuto. Aired October 24th, 2016.

original email: "We need to clean this up—[President Obama] has emails from her—they do not say state.gov."[230]   On October 28th, Federal Bureau of Investigations Director James Comey sent a letter to congressional leaders stating: "In connection with an unrelated case, the FBI has learned of the existence of emails that appear to be pertinent to the investigation [of former Secretary Clinton's personal email server.]"

On the same day that Director Comey sent the letter to congressional leaders, Congressman Issa again appeared on Your World with Neil Cavuto to discuss this issue. Neil Cavuto mentioned that no one in the State Department, the White House, or the Clinton campaign seemed to have been made aware of the letter before Director Comey sent it to congressional leaders. In reference to the WikiLeaks revelation on October 25th, Congressman Issa stated, "they probably were informed and we will find that out years from now." He then followed up with the question: "Four years after Hillary Clinton left office, why is it she has not turned over the documents she was required to leave at the State Department by law when she left?" Referring back to President Obama's comments in La Jolla, Congressman Issa said, "the

---

[230] Eder, Steve. "'We Need to Clean This Up': Clinton Aide's Newly Public Email Shows Concern." *New York Times*. October 25th, 2016.

fact that President Obama was emailing back and forth to her private email, and then he comes to my own district and says there has not been a single major scandal in his administration might be a better point. This is a major scandal, and it is a scandal of the making of Hillary Clinton."[231]

Throughout October, Congressman Issa appears to have landed a counter-punch after every punch thrown by Colonel Applegate, seemingly coordinated with the Trump campaign. When Colonel Applegate launched attack ads related to the September 11th Attacks, Congressman Issa countered with an endorsement from Rudy Giuliani. When Colonel Applegate attacked Congressman Issa over the Access Hollywood tape, Congressman Issa fired back with Colonel Applegate's divorce records. Although not planned, leaked emails from WikiLeaks and Director Comey's decision to re-open the investigation into former Secretary Clinton's private email server gave Congressman Issa the opportunity to criticize President Obama immediately after he claimed there had been no major scandals in his administration. By comparison, the Applegate

---

[231] Fox News: Your World with Neil Cavuto. Aired October 28th, 2016.

campaign often did not have a direct response to the attack ads released by the Issa campaign.

CHAPTER 8: THE FINAL STRETCH

In the last few days of October, Colonel Applegate seems to have focused exclusively on solidifying support among Democrats in the district. He attended a candidate forum hosted by the Democratic Party in Del Mar on October 26th and a forum hosted by the San Diego County Young Democrats on October 30th. The location of the second event was not actually in the district. Endorsements for Colonel Applegate in the closing days of the election came from leftwing political organizations. The Human Rights Campaign, which describes itself as "the largest national lesbian, gay, bisexual, transgender and queer civil rights organization," endorsed Colonel Applegate on October 26th. Congressman Issa's voting record had received a 32% score on the Human Rights Campaign report card.[232] End Citizens United, a political action committee established "to counter the disastrous effects of *Citizens United* and reform our campaign finance system," also endorsed Colonel Applegate, on October 31st.[233] The Applegate campaign released two ads in the final stretch of the campaign. One of them, titled "Still," was very similar to the previous commercial titled "Access." It used clips of the Access Hollywood tape and even also used the phrase "Say no to Donald Trump and Darrell Issa." The second commercial was titled "Face It." The commercial showed Colonel Applegate looking off into the distance. He narrated the commercial himself, saying, in part: "Let's face it, something's wrong. The system's broken. Congress is broken. Politicians? They don't represent us. It doesn't have to be this way."[234] Of these six activities to reach voters, five of them were targeted directly towards Democrats. Candidate forums hosted by political parties are likely to only be attended by the party

---

[232] Applegate for Congress Press Release: "Human Rights Campaign Endorses Colonel Doug Applegate for Congress." October 26th, 2016.

[233] Applegate for Congress Press Release: "End Citizens United Endorses Doug Applegate for Congress." October 31st, 2016.

[234] Applegate for Congress Press Release: "Colonel Applegate Releases Two New Ads: It's Time to Put Politics Aside and Put Country First." November 1st, 2016.

faithful. Voters influenced by the views of the Human Rights Campaign or End Citizens United were likely already Democrats. Assuming the Applegate campaign's messaging throughout the election had successfully linked Congressman Issa to Donald Trump, then the commercial "Still" was likely to not have any additional impact on voter perception. Although the commercial "Face It" was relatively non-partisan, it likely served as a reminder to Republicans in the district that congressional gridlock was the only way to limit a potential President Hillary Clinton. On November 4th, the California Democratic Party released television and radio ads featuring First Lady Michelle Obama. In them, she asked voters in San Diego to vote for Democrats in the upcoming election.[235] She did not specifically mention any candidate's name.

The Issa campaign released two commercials in the closing days of the election. The first, titled "Keeping Us Safe," featured Orange County Sheriff Sandra Hutchens and San Diego County Sheriff Bill Gore. Without going into details, the two sheriffs talked about Congressman Issa's support for "important laws that are keeping you safe," and his

---

[235] California Democratic Party Press Release: "New TV and Radio Ads: Michelle Obama Urges San Diegans to Vote." November 4th, 2016.

integrity. Sheriff Gore's last comment in the commercial was "Darrell Issa is our Congressman and we are proud of him." Sheriff Hutchens followed Sheriff Gore's statement with "And we need to keep him in Congress."[236] The second commercial was titled "Truth." It began with a clip of Colonel Applegate telling the Energy Upgrade California forum, "I have been a trial lawyer for three and a half decades." A voiceover then says he wants to raise taxes and slash military spending, without going into specifics. The narrator then says: "Applegate's personal behavior is even worse," claiming he treated a client unethically, was ordered to surrender his guns to the police, and was caught peeping into a woman's bedroom window. The commercial ends with another clip of Colonel Applegate at the forum saying: "I usually don't lead with that because I'm not going to get any votes."[237] On November 1st, the same day the Applegate campaign released a commercial attacking Congressman Issa for supporting the Trump campaign, Donald Trump tweeted: "@darrellissa is a very good man. Help him

---

[236] Issa for Congress Press Release: "New Ad: San Diego and Orange County Sheriffs Say We Need Congressman Darrell Issa." October 24th, 2016.

[237] Issa for Congress Press Release: "Issa Campaign Releases New Ad: 'Truth.'" October 25th, 2016.

win his congressional seat in California." November 1st also happened to be Congressman Issa's birthday, which he spent biking across the district, meeting with voters.[238] The next day, Congressman Issa received a major endorsement from General James F. Amos, the retired 35th Commandant of the Marine Corps. In the statement, General Amos said: "A tireless advocate for veterans, the 42,000 Marines and Sailors at Camp Pendleton, and their families, have an incomparable ally in Darrell Issa. America and its Marines need Darrell Issa in Congress."[239] The *Military Times* reported on the endorsement on November 5th, noting it "comes as a direct attack on one of the strengths of Issa's Democratic rival, retired Marine Corps Col. Doug Applegate, an Iraq War veteran."[240] On November 3rd, the Issa campaign announced an "It Takes Chutzpah" bus tour.[241] Between November 4th and November 7th,

---

[238] Panzar, Javier. "Darrell Issa 'Appreciates' Donald Trump's Twitter Shoutout." *Los Angeles Times*. November 1st, 2016.

[239] Issa for Congress Press Release: "35th Marine Corps Commandant James F. Amos Endorses Congressman Darrell Issa for Re-Election." November 2nd, 2016.

[240] Schogol, Jeff and Shane III, Leo. "Races to Watch: Former Commandant's Endorsement Goes Against Marine Vet Challenger." *Military Times*. November 5th, 2016.

[241] Issa for Congress Press Release: "Media Advisory: Issa for Congress Announces 'It Takes Chutzpah' Bus Tour." November 3rd, 2016.

Congressman Issa held campaign events at Iron Sights Shooting Range, Flying Pig Restaurant, Little Cakes Cupcake Kitchen, Belching Beaver Brewery, Vista Entertainment Center, Vista Farmers Market, Oceanside Pier, San Clemente Farmers Market, Carlsbad Village Street Faire, Dana Point Harbor, UFC Gym, Leap Coffee, Gunther Guns, Potato Shack Café, and Chief's Burgers. Overall, these final activities likely added support for Congressman Issa or reduced support for Colonel Applegate. His endorsements from the two county sheriffs and the former Commandant of the Marine Corps, which are officially non-partisan positions, likely increased support for Congressman Issa or decreased support for Colonel Applegate among undecided voters with a connection to Camp Pendleton. The anti-Applegate commercial likely caused some voters that marginally supported Colonel Applegate to doubt his character. Donald Trump's direct endorsement might have helped Congressman Issa win votes from pro-Trump voters that would have not voted for Republicans down the ballot. The bus tour events were largely non-partisan, thus allowing Congressman Issa to reach out to more swing voters.

Reuters/Ipsos, Economist/YouGov, and NBC News/Wall Street Journal conducted ten polls throughout October to gauge the nationwide partisan leanings in the upcoming congressional elections. On aggregate, Democrat candidates were favored by about 45% of respondents, whereas Republicans were favored by about 40% of respondents, representing a 5% lead. Republicans had their worst showing among 2,363 likely voters polled by Reuters/Ipsos in the early days of October. That poll showed Republicans trailing Democrats on the generic ballot by 10 points.[242] Republicans had their best showing among 1,000 registered voters polled by NBC News/Wall Street Journal in the middle of October. That poll showed Republicans only trailing Democrats on the generic ballot by 2 points.[243] Although Republicans were still losing, they were not losing as badly.

In last poll of the cycle, the Republican Party closed the gap significantly compared to October's results. The NBC News/Wall Street Journal Survey, taken from November 3rd to 5th, showed Democrats in the best position, with 47% of 1,282 likely voters favoring them in the upcoming election. Only 44% of respondents favored Republicans, giving the

---

[242] Reuters/Ipsos. "Core Political Data." Published October 11th, 2016.

[243] NBC News/Wall Street Journal Survey. Study #16991. Date Range: October 10th-13th, 2016.

Democrats a 3-point advantage.[244] The Economist/YouGov poll, taken from November 4th to 7th, found 45% of 3,677 likely voters favored a generic Democrat candidate for Congress, whereas only 42% of respondents favored a Republican candidate.[245] Although that is also a 3-point lead over Republicans, there were more uncertain voters than in the NBC News/Wall Street Journal Survey. The Reuters/Ipsos poll, which among the three polls was taken the furthest from Election Day, found that 42% of respondents favored a Democrat candidate, whereas 41% favored a Republican candidate. That gave Democrats only a 1-point advantage on the generic ballot. Combined, these three polls found that 44.67% of likely voters favored the Democratic Party on the generic ballot, whereas only 42.33% of likely voters favored the Republican Party. Although Democrat candidates held the lead, the gap had closed significantly. The closer it got to Election Day, the more voters swung towards the Republican Party in Congress. That might have been due to the expectation that Hillary Clinton would be elected president. The Economist/YouGov poll referenced above found that 9% of the electorate preferred the

---

[244] NBC News/Wall Street Journal Survey. Study #161256. Date Range: November 3rd-5th, 2016.

[245] Economist/YouGov Poll, conducted November 4th-7th, 2016.

White House and Congress be controlled by different parties. In a race that was determined by so few votes, the voters in the 49th Congressional District that prefer divided government might have expected Clinton to take the White House, and therefore vote for Congressman Issa with hopes of keeping a Republican-controlled Congress.

CHAPTER 9: ELECTION DAY

On Election Day, Congressman Issa received 50.3% of the vote, or 155,888 votes. Colonel Applegate received 154,267 votes, meaning Congressman Issa led the race with only 1,621 votes. Hillary Clinton received more votes than Donald Trump within the boundaries of the 49th Congressional District. She received 159,081 votes, or 50.7% of the vote. Donald Trump only received 135,576 votes, or 43.2% of the vote.[246] As was the case in the primary, Congressman Issa received more votes than Donald Trump and Colonel Applegate received fewer votes than Hillary Clinton in the 49th Congressional District. Interestingly, more votes

------

[246] California Secretary of State. "Supplement to the Statement of Vote: Counties by Congressional Districts for President." Certified December 18th, 2016.

were cast for the congressional candidates than the presidential candidates.

In the 2012 general election, Congressman Issa received 159,725 votes and his Democrat rival received 114,893 votes.[247] Before that election, there were 157,812 registered Republicans in the 49th Congressional District. By the 2016 general election, the number of registered Republicans in the district had declined by over 11,000. However, between the two elections, Congressman Issa's vote total only declined by 3,837 votes. Even though the Republican Party was losing registered voters, Congressman Issa managed to achieve victory by maintaining support from the majority of those ex-Republicans. Colonel Applegate increased his vote total by 39,374 votes, compared to the Democrat candidate in 2012. Registered Democrats in the district only increased by slightly over 11,000, meaning Colonel Applegate likely made up the balance by attracting voters not affiliated with either major party.

In the Post General Report to the Federal Election Commission, Applegate for Congress reported $1.9 million in total receipts and $1.8 million

---

[247] California Secretary of State. "Statement of the Vote." Certified December 14th, 2012.

in total disbursements throughout the election.[248] Issa for Congress reported $2.5 million in total receipts and $5.9 million in total disbursements throughout the election.[249] To win the election by 1,621 votes, Issa for Congress had to spend $4.9 million more than Applegate for Congress. On a per vote basis, that represents a marginal cost of $3,022.83 per vote.

Throughout California, Hillary Clinton received more votes than Donald Trump in seven congressional districts that re-elected Republicans, including the 49th Congressional District. However, in six of those districts, the Republican candidate received more votes than Hillary Clinton. Even if every Democrat congressional candidate had equivalent support as Hillary Clinton, they would still lose against the Republican incumbent. Congresswoman Mimi Walters and Congressman Dana Rohrabacher both received 20,000 more votes than Hillary Clinton in their own districts. Donald Trump's performance on a congressional district basis is not an accurate reflection of the strength of the California Republican Party.

---

[248] Filing FEC-1153944. FEC Form 3: Post-General. Amendment 1. Filed March 24th, 2017.
[249] Filing FEC-1141882. FEC Form 3: Post-General. Amendment 1. Filed January 26th, 2017.

Because of California's top-two primary system, there were nine congressional districts that did not have a Republican candidate on the ballot. Despite not having a Republican congressional candidate, a Republican senatorial candidate, or a reasonable probability of flipping the state's Electoral College votes, there were still over 300,000 people that cast ballots for Donald Trump in those districts.

Despite the media speculating that Donald Trump would have a negative impact on Republican turnout while energizing Democrats, results in the 49th Congressional District indicate otherwise. As was mentioned previously, the number of registered Republicans in the district declined by more than 11,000 voters between presidential elections, but Donald Trump received 1,129 more votes in the district than Mitt Romney did. Despite the number of registered Democrats in the district increasing by more than 11,000 voters between presidential elections, Hillary Clinton only received 5,225 more votes in the district than President Obama did.

There seems to have been an expectation that voters would punish Republicans due to their support for Donald Trump. The opposite seems to have occurred. All Republican congressional incumbents in California were re-elected. Two Republican congressional incumbents in California besides Congressman Issa were also targeted: Jeff Dunham in the 10th Congressional District and Steve Knight in the 25th Congressional District. Both of them received more votes than the Republican candidate for those offices did in 2012, when Mitt Romney was on the ticket. Donald Trump received more votes in the 10th Congressional District than Mitt Romney did. Both candidates received more votes than Hillary Clinton did in their district.

There is the curious case of Encinitas Mayor Kristin Gaspar, candidate for the San Diego County Board of Supervisors. On the day of the primary, Mayor Gaspar said in a television interview: "I cast a vote for Trump today. I think that it is important that we have someone that moves forward with Republican principles, and that is why I cast the vote the way that I did."

She later revoked her support for Donald Trump after the Access Hollywood tape, but that interview clip never went away during the campaign. She defeated the Democrat incumbent.

Incumbent Republican Assemblywoman Young Kim lost re-election. She had refused to endorse Donald Trump. Assemblywoman Ling Ling Chang lost the contest to represent the 29th State Senate District. She had openly denounced Donald Trump. Losing these two districts caused the

California Republican Party to become a super minority in the state government. Sheriff Scott Jones challenged incumbent Democrat Congressman Ami Bera for California's 7th Congressional District, but lost with only 48.8% of the vote. Sheriff Jones had revoked his endorsement of Donald Trump after the Access Hollywood video. Instead of rewarding Republican politicians for distancing themselves from Donald Trump, voters actually punished them.

Despite Hillary Clinton winning California with 62.2% of the vote, which was higher than President Obama's lead in 2012, there was no impact on the Congressional delegation's partisan composition. The first reason is that California's delegation is already dis-proportionately tilted towards the Democratic Party. Donald Trump received 31.8% of the vote, but Republicans only hold 26.4% of Congressional seats in California. Second, Hillary Clinton did well in places that already overwhelmingly supported the Democratic Party. The median vote total for Hillary Clinton in all 53 congressional districts was about 160,000 votes. Hillary Clinton received more than 300,000 votes in the 12th Congressional District, which was a 39,000 vote increase over President Obama in 2012. Congresswoman Nancy Pelosi, the House Minority

Leader during the 2016 election, represents the 12th Congressional District.

A similar phenomenon caused Hillary Clinton to lose the election nationwide. The Associated Press determined Hillary Clinton won 2.9 million more votes than Donald Trump nationwide in the 2016 election.[250] She won California with 4.2 million more votes than Donald Trump, meaning she lost the rest of the country by 1.3 million votes. The geographic distribution of Hillary Clinton's support also impacted the U.S. Senate. Republican incumbent senators in Pennsylvania and Wisconsin likely won re-election on Donald Trump's coattails in those states. This meant the U.S. Senate would have 52 Republicans and 48 Democrats. If those two races had turned out differently, the U.S. Senate would have been split 50-50. In the House of Representatives, Hillary Clinton was not able to convert her popular vote victory into a Democrat majority. Republican candidates actually received more than one million more votes than Democrat candidates, and maintained a 47-seat majority.[251]

---

[250] Lerer, Lisa. "Clinton Wins Popular Vote by Nearly 2.9 Million." Associated Press. December 22nd, 2016.

[251] Leamon, Eileen and Bucelato, Jason. "Election Results for the U.S. President, the U.S. Senate, and the U.S. House of

Congresswoman Pelosi had predicted Democrats would pick up 20 seats in the House, but only picked up six. The Red to Blue Program, which eventually included the 49th Congressional District, successfully flipped only seven of its original 31 targets. That is a 22.6% success rate.

Because the 49th Congressional District election was so close, the results would not be known for weeks after Election Day. On November 28th, Congressman Issa declared victory after the Associated Press called the race in his favor.[252] On December 2nd, Colonel Applegate announced his intention to run for Congress in 2018.[253] Thus concluded the closest race of 2016.

Representatives." Federal Election Commission. December, 2017. Page 11.

[252] Issa for Congress Press Release: "Issa Statement on Re-Election Win." November 28th, 2016.

[253] Applegate for Congress Press Release: "Applegate Statement on Election Results." December 2nd, 2016.